Absolute Beginner Series....

Write Your Book!
Publish Your Book!
Market Your Book!

*People, Pointers, and Products
To Make Your Book REAL*

by

Blythe Ayne

Absolute Beginner Series:

Write Your Book! Publish Your Book! Market Your Book!
People, Pointers, and Products to Make Your Book REAL
Blythe Ayne

Emerson & Tilman, Publishers
129 Pendleton Way #55
Washougal, WA 98671

All Rights Reserved
No part of this publication may be reproduced, distributed, or transmitted
in any form, or by any means, including photocopying, recording,
or other electronic or mechanical methods, without the prior
written permission of the author, except brief quotations
in critical reviews and other noncommercial
uses permitted by copyright law.

Thank you Pixabay for generously sharing your inspiring graphics

www.BlytheAyne.com

Write Your Book! Publish Your Book! Market Your Book!
People, Pointers, and Products to Make Your Book REAL
(Book 1 in the Absolute Beginner Series)
ISBN: 978-1-947151-51-2

[1. LANGUAGE ARTS & DISCIPLINES / Publishing
2. LANGUAGE ARTS & DISCIPLINES / Authorship
3. BUSINESS & ECONOMICS / E-Commerce / General**]** *I. Title*
BIC: FM
First Edition

Absolute Beginner Series....

Write Your Book!
Publish Your Book!
Market Your Book!

People, Pointers, and Products To Make Your Book REAL

by

Blythe Ayne

Books & Audio by Blythe Ayne

Nonfiction:
Love Is The Answer
45 Ways To Excellent Life
Life Flows on the River of Love
Horn of Plenty–The Cornucopia of Your Life
Finding Your Path, Engaging Your Purpose

How to Save Your Life Series:
Save Your Life With The Power Of pH Balance
Save Your Life With The Phenomenal Lemon
Save Your Life with Stupendous Spices

Absolute Beginner Series:
Write Your Book! Publish Your Book! Market Your Book!

Fiction:
The Darling Undesirables Series:
The Heart of Leo - short story prequel
The Darling Undesirables
Moons Rising
The Inventor's Clone
Heart's Quest

Children's Illustrated Books:
The Rat Who Didn't Like Rats
The Rat Who Didn't Like Christmas

Short Story Collections:
5 Minute Stories
Lovely Frights for Lonely Nights

Poetry:
Home & the Surrounding Territory

CD:
The Power of pH Balance –
Dr. Blythe Ayne Interviews Steven Acuff

Physical books & ebooks are found wherever books are sold
Visit Blythe's Gumroad store: https://gumroad.com/Blythe

DEDICATION:

*To all the writers who share the heart of hope,
The love of creation,
& who often keep their candles burning
Long into the night.*

Table of Contents

Introduction	1
Write Your Book!	**5**
Jumping-Off Place	10
FICTION—I'm Stuck!	11
NONFICTION — I'm Stuck!	22
Editor, Proofreader	34
Pantsers Vs. Plotters	36
Stories Have Structure	39
Publish Your Book!	**47**
Your Website	47
Wordpress	48
Your Cover	51
A Word (Okay, a Bunch of Words) About ISBNs	52
Off to Amazon!	55
Kobo	58
iBooks	58
Nook	59
Ingram Spark/Lightning Source	60
Wattpad	61
Aggregators	63
Subscription Services	67
A Storefront of Your Own	70
Audiobooks	74
Help Getting Published	77
Editors & Proofreaders	77
Cover Artists	78
Virtual Assistants	78
Watching Out for Writers	80
Market Your Book!	**83**
Your List	83
Your Book Launch	93
Dynamic Ad Activity	95
General Internet Presence	103
Various Sites to Advertise Your Book	104
Helpful Indie Authors Blogs & Podcasts	108
Reviews	113
In Closing	115
References & Resources	118
About the Author	120

*"Writing is show business for shy people.
That's how I see it."*
Lee Child

Introduction

Writers are no longer constrained by a narrow, subjective, quarter-twain bottleneck in the river of publication, commandeered by a handful of people determining if our work will ever see the light of day.

Our *readers* support our writing—and not only by buying it, but by writing us and letting us know what they love in our stories, or what has helped them in our non-fiction books.

* *

I write fiction and nonfiction. I also write genre fiction and literary fiction. I've written under my legal name, a variety of pen names, and I've done an absolute plethora of ghost writing. I've been "traditionally published" by established publishers, and I've been published widely in the small press, alternate press/underground press scene.

But since the world began to spin a different direction, with self-publishing now significantly and viably upon the scene, I've become an "Indie Author."

I've become an indie author with boundless joy and a song in my heart. I no longer spend hours and hours poring over lists of publishers and agents, with yet more hours producing cover letters, synopses, and partials. I no longer send out dozens of submissions to get a small handful of acceptances, a larger handful of rejections, and even larger pile of no response whatsoever, for my precious time spent feeding a black hole.

Nor do I now go to writer's conferences in the hopes of "landing a deal." Now when I go to a conference, it's to hang out with writerly peers and enjoy myself, to glean and to share information about the current cutting edge of the publishing world—which is changing virtually daily.

As an indie author I'm in the awesome and delightful position of interacting directly with my readers. I get to discover for myself what strikes a resonating chord with them, instead of hoping a publisher and its team will find my readership.

Think about this my friend, we have the amazing privilege of interacting personally, one-on-one, with the people who have discovered our writing, who are delighted to be able to communicate with the author of the stories and the information that has touched their lives.

We live in astounding times!

Write Your Book!

But no good story is without challenges. All that I mention as *heaven* is also a bumpy road.

You are responsible to produce your book. No one is going to do it but you. You have to provide your own deadlines, and you must meet them. No one—*but you*—will demand that you turn in your manuscript.

You must learn how to use the software to manifest your beautiful book, or, conversely, sort out who does the work you need done, and hire them to do it. But the good news is that you can, indeed, farm out most of this work to people who have learned the various skills you may be lacking.

The less-good news is you still need to know the basics of those skills in order to retain the assistant (who may be a "virtual assistant" and very possibly, even probably, in some other part of our ever-shrinking world) who will best fulfill your needs. You need to know what's an appropriate fee, which you'll learn by experiencing, first hand, how much work is involved in the numerous aspects of orchestration required to produce a book.

In short, you need at least a working knowledge of the software products used to create a book, to interact meaningfully with the person you've retained to turn your manuscript into a book.

Once you have your book—whether an ebook or physical book or both, whether you're also including an audio book, whether you've manifested these forms yourself or have employed an assistant or assistants to help with this production—you must then find your readers. Or, more to the point, learn how your readers can *discover you*.

I'm not going to lie. This is hard work! And not only a lot of hard work, but a lot of *different kinds* of hard work.

However, in *Write Your Book! Publish Your Book! Market Your Book!* you'll find relevant, succinct, cutting-edge help in those three major fields—writing, publishing, marketing—where you must learn the game in order to have your unique, one-and-only, only-you-can-write-it, book in the hands of the people who are, even now, looking for it (not yet realizing it), when they scan the millions of published books.

*"You **are** a start-up ...*
The next great business is you."
Hugh Howey

Be a Part of the Indie Movement

So, dear peer writer, come join me. Be a part of the Indie Movement.

The ever-growing and successful Indie Movement has shown that we writers do, indeed, know what people want to read. We're proving we are capable of producing intriguing and significant—not-hashed-to-death by a cadre of agents, editors and marketers—writing.

That's not to disparage agents and editors of traditional publishing. Many of the wise among them are discovering meaningful work, hired directly by authors, engaging their skills to improve our work. But according to *our* specifications, not the specs of a marketing team who may never even meet or talk with the author.

I'm not suggesting that you don't consider traditional publishing. But I *am* suggesting that you become an indie author to have both the psychological and objective power in the game. That is to say, publish and prove yourself so that the traditional publisher *comes to you*, rather than the other way around. This is as it ought to be.

It becomes more and more true that publishers must play nice or authors will simply produce their work without them. The tables have turned. Authors no longer have to approach publishers and agents, hat in hand, in supplication.

Let's Dive In

Come along with me as I take you into what I've learned writing and studying the Indie Movement, and let me save you mountains of time in the process.

I've also included information about some of the most successful indie authors, who are magnanimous and expansive in sharing their experiences, knowledge, and wisdom. In the indie environment you'll often hear, "A rising tide lifts all boats."

The Indie Movement is not only awe-inspiring, it is truly world changing.

The Nitty Gritty

Have you written your book? Do you feel confident that it's ready for publication? If so, you may want to move ahead to the *Publish Your Book* section. If you feel doubtful, then read the rest of this chapter.

If you haven't finished your book yet, where are you stuck? The rubber hits the road right here, right now. Answer the following questions to get a ground-zero perspective of where you are, as that's the only place from which you can move. Be brutally honest.

Make a note of the statements that indicate your current status in your book-writing process.

Jumping-Off Place

1. 🔲 I don't have an idea yet for a book, but I've always wanted to write.

2. 🔲 I haven't written a book, but I have an idea.
   🔲 It's Fiction   🔲 It's Nonfiction

3. 🔲 My idea is in my mind. I've not yet committed it to paper.

4. 🔲 I've scribbled some notes about my plot/story, but it isn't exactly clear to me yet.
   🔲 I've scribbled some notes about my nonfiction idea, but they're not organized.

5. Groundwork:
🔲 I've done some research for my book.
🔲 I interviewed an expert or someone of interest.
🔲 I traveled or _____ (some other bit of work) investigating my story/topic.

6. 🔲 I Feel like I'm *All Systems Go!*

7. 🔲 I'm *Stuck!*

Maybe you're finding it hard to start. *You are not alone.* But *why* are you having trouble starting? Following are some statements to help you sort out where the *stuck* place is, note any of the comments that ring true for you.

Give yourself a week to let the answers to the following questions "incubate" while the little birdie of your book takes form in its creative egg.

We'll start with fiction, then move to nonfiction.

FICTION—I'm Stuck!

▥ I have an idea, but when I try to write it, I realize it's not enough for a book.

▥ I know what the story is, but I can't seem to write the first sentence.

▥ I have a story, but I can't get a bead on the protagonist.

▥ I have a fascinating character, but I'm not sure what the story is.

▥ Although I'd really love to "be a writer," when I sit down to write, I hear an inner monologue that goes something like, "who do you think you are? You're not a writer. No one will be interested in the story you have to write."

▥ I have no idea why I don't start writing. I just know that when I sit down to write, suddenly the floors need to be mopped, or boxes of stuff in the garage I haven't looked at in years need to be sorted, or some-such distraction takes me away from writing.

📓 Maybe I'm stuck because

_____

_____

_____

Every problem has a solution, and each of the foregoing barriers to getting your book written has a solution. Let's dig a bit further into the fiction writing impediments.

📓 I have an idea, but when I try to write, I realize it's not enough for a book.

If you have an idea but it's not enough for a book, spend half-an-hour every day for the next seven days writing down ideas that may—or may not—go along with your original idea.

It doesn't matter if they're bad ideas, or weird ideas, or ideas that seem unrelated to your original idea. You're brainstorming. All's fair in love and brainstorming.

There's only one rule:

𝔗𝔥𝔬𝔲 𝔖𝔥𝔞𝔩𝔱 𝔑𝔬𝔱 𝔍𝔲𝔡𝔤𝔢 𝔄𝔫𝔶 𝔬𝔣 𝔱𝔥𝔢 𝔍𝔡𝔢𝔞𝔰 𝔗𝔥𝔞𝔱 ℭ𝔬𝔪𝔢 𝔉𝔬𝔯𝔱𝔥 𝔦𝔫 𝔅𝔯𝔞𝔦𝔫𝔰𝔱𝔬𝔯𝔪𝔦𝔫𝔤

Your occupation, for the moment, is simply to function as court reporter—to record what comes up, nothing more. But it *is* your job to do this every day for half-an-hour, for *the next seven days*. No, you may not put this off until some future time when something-something-something is different, or more convenient, or better.

DO NOT read what you wrote until after your seventh day session.

Yes, you read that correctly. No reading what you wrote. The subconscious mind is wonderfully full of answers to the questions we ask, but we are far too inclined to stop it down with our mulling and critiquing. Leave the seeds alone so they can germinate. Come to your half-hour session and write, then move away from it.

This exercise works miraculously. At the end of seven days you'll likely have *pages* of half-baked but intriguing ideas, ripe concepts, compelling thoughts, curious musings, etc., etc., etc., from which you can begin to build the scaffolding of your book.

I know what the story is, but I can't seem to write the first sentence.

Then **don't** write the first sentence. Write some other sentence. Write a sentence from the middle of the book. Write the second sentence. Write a sentence that you would send in an email to a friend, telling her about your book. Write a sentence for the back of the book, or the book's Amazon/Kobo/iBooks description, or your website blurb, or the book's landing page teaser.

Most writers have no idea what the first sentence of a book is until having written some, or maybe all, of the book. If the first sentence feels daunting, that's no surprise. After all, the whole book comes after that first sentence. You're right, it's extremely important. Just begin to write the rest of the book and leave the first sentence alone if it's troubling you or impeding you.

You might be surprised to wake up in the middle of the night, some night, with the first sentence in your mind, crystal clear as if etched on glass. *NOW*, write your first sentence down. You think you'll remember it. *You will not*. Write it down or record it on your phone, or send it to yourself in an email. Whatever you do, get it down.

📖 I have a story, but I can't get a bead on the protagonist I must confess, this is a problem that's difficult for me to relate to. I usually have a character demanding to be given life before all else.

But, if this *were* my problem, I'll share with you my process to become acquainted with minor characters, which works like a charm to make them come alive, and I believe it will work if your protagonist is not coming clear for you—you can try this approach to see if it works.

Write a character sketch answering the following questions:

Given the story that's in my mind, what are some general details of a person living the life I'm about to give to this character?

What does my protagonist do for a living?

What are my protagonist's hobbies, avocations, skills, talents?

What is my character's ethnic/cultural background, hair, eye, skin coloring, body type, height, weight, and age?

Does my protagonist have a significant other? What are a few details about this person?

What's a detail about my protagonist that evokes sympathy? What's a detail that evokes criticism or judgment?

What is a detail about my protagonist that no one else in the story world knows, and may never know, but that contributes to my understanding of my protagonist's character, motivations, and personality?

How did my protagonist become involved in the story events—*before its beginning*?

After answering these questions—as well as any other questions and details that arise in the process—I then need a flesh-and-blood person to attach the attributes to. If someone I know hasn't come to mind, I'll go out and people watch, hunkering down in a corner of a restaurant or coffee shop. Or I'll go to an event where I can watch the flow of humanity interacting with one another.

As I quietly observe, someone will suddenly step right into my character's lifeless body and animate it. A tilt of the head, a quality of voice, a ... whatever ... *something* triggers the synapses and all the components tumble into place—the beautiful Frankenstein arises.

Maybe some—*maybe many!*—of the things in your sketch about your character will change when this flesh-and-blood person triggers your creativity, which is fine. The only thing that matters is to have a living, breathing, fascinating, *someone*. Unique. Distinct. Intriguing.

Because you will never have a story if it's not driven by a real, flesh and blood—or whatever it's made of—*being*. As a human, what you know about, since you are one, is humans. Even if your character is a demon or an angel, an alien or a pixie, she will ultimately become animate by the breath of life you exhale into her from your own *human* knowledge and experience.

I cannot overstate the importance of a well-developed protagonist. To write the tens of thousands of words that is a novel, you must have a dimensional, fascinating character to carry you through those isolated days and nights when it's just you and your protagonist.

That's not to say your character won't surprise you. Quite the contrary. After breathing life into your character, she will, sooner or later, take on a life of her own, and, on occasion, seemingly take control of your fingers (or voice) to tell her story.

> *"Let the world burn through you.*
> *Throw the prism light, white hot, on paper."*
> **Ray Bradbury**

◼ I have a fascinating character, but I'm not sure what the story is.

Yay! You're intrigued by a dimensional, engaging character, so much that you want to write his story. But what is it?

What's especially great about this creative jumping-off place is that a fascinating character, capable of doing anything in the universe you're about to construct, has excellent potential for a series before you even begin.

This is another half-an-hour for seven days exercise. It's potentially so much fun because there are no boundaries. Half-an-hour every day for the next seven days write down situations your protagonist might get into, note other characters who come on the scene, toy with the world you're building.

Anything goes!

What does your character enjoy doing, what is frustrating? What's your character's angst, joy, secret? What's at stake? What's the goal? What's between your character and this goal? What is your character's heart's desire? What are self-limiting beliefs?

What will your protagonist come to know, learn, realize by the end of the book, that changes his personality, character, beliefs, behaviors, and outlook from who he was at the beginning?

Whatever the fantastic trappings may be, whatever the original ideas, the fabulous backdrop, the unbelievable story, *readers read novels to be informed about the human condition.*

We have, for eons, sat huddled around fires, keeping the dark of night at bay, listening with rapt attention to the story teller. We come back every night because we want to be titillated, entertained, given a fright, taken on a journey, gain insight into how to handle life situations, or learn about love. We want to feel sad, anxious, angry, happy, relieved.

We've hunkered down with story tellers because they make us shed tears, they make us laugh, they make us think, they let us feel. They help us realize that we are not alone, while we share, in the landscape of our mind, the character's story.

Story tellers have been, and remain, the protectors and advancers of culture, of civilization. They clarify evil and wrong-doing, they teach us about love.

Whenever someone says to me (as people far too often do), "I don't read fiction," I answer, "there's no such thing as fiction," by which I mean that although people and places may be made up, essential human truths are brought to light in "fiction," sometimes more concretely, more wisely, and more revealing, than in nonfiction.

Fiction is the "safe place" where we look at ourselves with all our faults, foibles, limitations, idiosyncrasies, secrets, sins and self-abuse. It's where we learn about the human family's folkways and mores, where we gain insights into our courage, sacrifices, perseverance, purpose, patience, dedication, serenity and love.

> *"It may be fiction, but it has to be true."*
> **Jacquelyn Mitchard**

Although I'd really love to "be a writer," when I sit down to write, an inner monologue goes something like, "who do you think you are?"

Fear of failure and fear of success can make the fascinating characters in your mind recede and the story seem irrelevant. I've written at length about this in an article; *Fear of Failure, Fear of Success – Fated Twins or Helpful Teammates?* (BlytheAyne.com/FearofFailure). These twin bugaboos cripple many artistic endeavors.

Fear of failure dictates that we'd better succeed, or we'll look like an idiot in front of all the people we told we were writing a book.

At the same time, fear of success freezes us. Perhaps you start to think, "What if my book is a success? I'll have to do all the things writers do when they have a successful book, won't I? I'll have to give readings and go to book signings and … whatever. I'll have to *talk* in front of *people!* I don't think I can pull that off."

Or maybe you think, "I really don't want to do all that glad-handing. I'm an introvert (most writers are). I just want to write."

Another fear of success litany is, "I'm a sham. I'm not really a writer. If my book is a success, I'll be exposed as the deceiver that I am."

I've worked with a number of clients who desired to write (I was a psychotherapist in private practice for twenty-plus years), and I also have friends and acquaintances who long to be writers. When I ask "how's the book coming along?" I'll hear some form of one of the above litanies, those crippling excuses, 9.5 times out of 10.

So, you're not alone. But this is my suggestion—thumb your nose at fears. Move intrepidly ahead and create the worlds and people that only you can create.

When the little voice asks, "Who do you think you are?" Answer, "never mind who I think I am. It only matters *that I write*. I'm putting on my white-noise headphones, and I'm writing. *You can't stop me, little voice, I can't hear you!*"

I have no idea why I don't start writing. I just know that when I sit down to write, the floors need to be mopped, or stuff needs to be sorted.

It seems that there's no better way to get ugly tasks done than to sit down to write. I guess that's a small bonus, getting ugly, non-writing, tasks done. But that's not what this book is about.

This book is about *getting your book written!*

This challenge of distractions must be dealt with firmly. A beginning approach is to make a bargain with that "urgent stuff." Make it a simple contract, and stick to it. For instance, you might say to yourself, "I will 'get to' mop the floor after I've written five-hundred words. They don't have to be the most amazing words, but there has to be at least five-hundred of them, and they must be either a part of the novel, or directly related to the work I'm doing with my novel."

When you take a firm hand with the noise of the subconscious—which will almost always resist doing something new—you'll discover that the floor-mopping, box-sorting, becomes less and less urgent as you sit down to write.

The noise of these distractions even begins to completely disappear when the thrill of creating outweighs everything else. You'll arrive at the place where you wish the world would just go away and let you write!

Gradually, the subconscious becomes recruited, as it learns how satisfying and pleasurable your work is.

📓 Maybe I'm stuck because
_____
_____
_____

I'm super interested in what you might write here, if you have an idea about your challenges that are different from the other possibilities considered. If you want to share what you wrote, please do.
Write to me: Blythe@BlytheAyne.com

> *"Tomorrow may be hell,*
> *but today was a good writing day,*
> *and on the good writing days*
> *nothing else matters."*
> Neil Gaiman

NONFICTION — I'm Stuck

Now, for those of you writing a nonfiction book, let's consider what may be getting between you and your published book, over there on the shelf. I can just see it, can't you?

Check any of the boxes that are a fit regarding your current challenges, and let's take a look at ways to set these obstructions aside.

☐ I have an idea, but when I try to write, I realize it's not enough for a book.

☐ I know the subject matter of my book, but I can't seem to write the first sentence.

☐ I know the subject matter, but I can't imagine how to organize it.

📖 Although I'd really love to "be a writer," when I sit down to write, I hear an inner monologue that says, "who do you think you are? You're not a writer. No one will be interested in the book you have to write."

📖 I have no idea why I don't start writing. I just know that when I sit down to write, suddenly I must get the car's oil changed, or the lawn must be mowed, or some-such distraction takes me away from writing.

📖 Maybe I'm stuck because

_____

_____

_____

Let's consider these statements, one by one:

📖 I have an idea, but when I try to write, I realize it's not enough for a book.

I'll bet your idea *is* enough for a book.

Go to Amazon, type your subject in the search bar and see what comes up. With its millions of books, it's just about certain that there are books on your subject, or a tangential subject, that gets your creative juices flowing, and helps you see directions you might take to grow your idea.

If, in doing this, you become discouraged and feel, well, my book has already been written, fear not—*your book has not been written until you write it.*

Do you have any idea how many books there are like this one you are reading now? A slew! A veritable slew. But here you are, reading this one. It might be because you've read other books on the subject and want to read everything you can find on the topic, or it might be that you've stumbled upon my book first and haven't yet seen the others.

Whatever the case, no two books—even on the same subject—are the same. You have your experience, your insights, your knowledge, your driving inspiration, and the groundwork you've done. Together, these facts, these features, make your book unique. You have a way of communicating that will resonate, *just so*, with your readers, who, as I already mentioned, are looking for your book, though they may not yet know it.

Whether in development or completed, your book is unique. You may be inspired by other writers in your niche, but you have your spin, you have your particular mix of knowledge and wisdom, you have your original ideas. And most precious of all, you have your voice. *Only you have your voice.*

If there really are no books on your subject, boy, I'd like to know what your subject is. If this is true, though, I'd suggest that you focus on a related subject that *does* have a few books in its corner, just to get your book-writing experience into motion. Consider writing a short book on this more familiar topic, and, meanwhile, you can flesh out your "totally original book" in your mind and in notes, preparing it for its debut.

Further, I suggest you take on the exercise I gave to the fiction writers. Spend half-an-hour every day for the next seven days writing down ideas that may be the same, or may be different, from your central germ of an idea.

It doesn't matter if they're bad ideas, or weird ideas, or ideas that are, as I say, not particularly related to your original idea. It's brainstorming. To repeat, all's fair in love and brainstorming.

And there remains but one rule:

Thou Shalt Not Judge Any of the Ideas That Come Forth in Brainstorming

You write what comes up, every day for half-an-hour, for the next seven days. You may not put it off until some future time when the stars are realigned. *You start now.*

Furthermore, DO NOT read what you wrote until after the seventh session. The subconscious mind is stunningly equipped to provide answers to the questions we ask, but we often quash it with critiques. Leave the seeds alone to germinate. Come to your half-hour session and write, then move away from it.

At the end of seven days you'll have *pages* of fascinating ideas, original concepts, boggling thoughts, marvelous musings, so on and so on and so forth, to begin to construct your book.

I know the subject matter of my book, but I can't seem to write the first sentence.

Just as I suggested to fiction authors, if the first sentence isn't coming clear in your mind, ***don't*** write the first sentence. Write some other sentence. Write a sentence from the middle of the book. Write the second sentence. Write a sentence that you would send in an email to a friend about your book. Write a sentence for the back of the book, or the book's publisher detail page, or your website blurb, or the book's landing page teaser.

As previously mentioned, most writers have no idea what the first sentence of a book is until having written some, or maybe all, of the book. If the first sentence feels daunting, that's no surprise. The whole book comes after that first sentence, and it *is* very important. Begin to write the rest of the book, until the first sentence comes to you.

And it will. You'll wake up in the middle of the night some night, or be at a restaurant with some friends, or engaged in some other activity, and the first sentence will leap into your mind, crystal clear, etched on glass, demanding to be written. *NOW*, write your first sentence down. You think you'll remember it. *You will not*. Write it down immediately. Or record it on your phone, or send it to yourself in an email. Just get it down.

▪ I know the subject matter, but I can't imagine how to organize it.

I'm writing in Scrivener. Yay, Scrivener. A fabulous organizing tool. It's usual to be challenged by all the materials and insights and research and references and quotes and whatever else you might have in your nonfiction work (fiction too, by the way).

Scrivener is an *amazing* tool, developed for both Mac and PC platforms, and only costs $45, I believe. After I accomplished my word count for NaNoWriMo, it was half price.

An incredible bargain, at half or full price. It's more tool than you're likely ever to use, but what you *will* use, you'll love. You can make containers of each of your chapters and place bits and pieces, notes and thoughts in them if you so desire, or just write, full steam ahead.

You can put notes or snippets or what-have-you on the virtual cork board, on 3" x 5" virtual note cards, color code them, move them around. You can make footnotes that always stick where you want them to stick, no matter how much you move the text about.

You can put art, photos, graphics, charts, etc., etc., in the research file to place, when the time comes, in the text. You can put notes in the notes files and ideas in the ideas file.

Or none of that, as it suits you. It's inspiring and exciting what you can do with this flexible, time-and-sanity-saving tool. If you don't have it, you'll be glad you got it.

Go to LiteratureandLatte.com, the home of Scrivener to learn more and to purchase. I'm not an affiliate (though it appears I ought to be), I just believe in this tool, and I believe you'll be glad you have it.

All righty, so, what I'm saying is, first things first. Just dig in, gather information, write sections, take notes, talk to people, visit places, take pictures and write more notes—throw it all into Scrivener. Move parts about to see how the work is shaping up, and be happy in the knowledge that as you work and finesse and think and gather and write—your book, *miraculously!* takes shape under your hands.

You needn't take only my word for it. As you listen to the podcasts and read the blogs and emails of successful writers, you'll hear echoes of what I'm writing here.

With the next three statements I'm going to basically quote my fiction responses:

Although I'd really love to "be a writer," when I sit down to write, an inner monologue goes something like, "who do you think you are?"

Fear of failure and fear of success can make the enthralling material of your book grow small and seem irrelevant. I've written at length about these fears—which can cripple many artistic endeavors—in my article, *Fear of Failure, Fear of Success – Fated Twins or Helpful Teammates?* (BlytheAyne.com/FearofFailure).

Fear of failure dictates that if you don't succeed you'll look like an idiot in front of all the people you've told about the great book you're writing.

While fear of success can freeze you in your tracks. Perhaps you ask yourself, "what if my book *is* a success? Will I have to do all the things writers do when they have a successful book? Will I have to run around giving readings and going to book signings and … whatever?"

Perhaps you're thinking, "I'm posing myself as an expert, but am I? For sure there are many people who know more than I do about my subject. I'll be exposed for a charlatan. I'll never be able to pull it off!"

Or maybe you're musing, "I don't want to do all that running around, acting like I'm really enjoying it, when one thing I hate is to have to make small talk. I just want to write."

I've worked with a number of clients, and I have friends and acquaintances who are, or who desire to be, writers. When I ask them any variation of "how's the book coming along?" I hear one form or another of the foregoing self-produced barriers.

You're not alone—but turn your back on those niggling fears. You're going to create a wonderful book that the world has been waiting for. Your book will find its niche, and when that little voice asks you, "who do you think you are?" just answer, "don't ask who I am, ask what I've created. I scoff at you, little niggling, negative voice. There's no place for you here!"

📓 I have no idea why I don't start writing. I just know that when I sit down to write, the car suddenly must have its oil changed, or the lawn needs to be mowed.

It bears repeating, "There's no better way to get ugly tasks done than to sit down to write." Despite the small bonus in getting ugly tasks done, this book is about *getting your book written*.

The challenge of distractions must be dealt with firmly. A way to start is to make a bargain with those urgent, disruptive, tasks.

Make a simple contract with yourself and stick to it. You might say or think to yourself: "I will 'get to' change the oil in the car or mow the lawn, *after* I've written five-hundred words. They don't have to be the most amazing words, but there has to be five-hundred of them that are part of, or related to, my book."

Taking a firm hand a few times with the dictates of the subconscious as it resists doing something new—the subconscious fears and opposes new things—you'll discover that the oil changing or lawn mowing becomes less and less important when you sit down to write.

In fact, you'll look forward to the times you take yourself into your writing, and the urgency of those distractions will become very small, and even disappear, as the thrill of creating outweighs everything else.

Trust me, the moment will come when you wish the world would just go away and let you write!

🔲 Maybe I'm stuck because
_____
_____
_____

I'm curious about your insights if you've written something here. If you'd care to share, write me at: Blythe@BlytheAyne.com

Seven Days

Whether writing a novel or a nonfiction book, you now have a week's worth of solid contemplation, mind-mapping, blockage removal, notes and inspirations to nurture your work.

The time has arrived to begin writing your book (if you haven't gotten so inspired in the last week that you've "cheated" and begun to write it already).

Now is the time. Today is the day.

Moving Forward

Perhaps you're farther along than the foregoing contemplations. Where are you on these following measures?:

▪ I've produced an outline or similar document as a guide to begin writing my book. I consider this outline or script to be:

▪ Sketchy—it needs more before I'll feel like I can launch into my book.

▪ Fairly fleshed out. I'm almost ready to start.

▪ It's everything I need to get in motion—I'm ready to go.

▪ I have a working title for my book, and here it is:
_____

Return to the Jumping-Off Place

9. Your Book in the 3-Dimensions:

▪ I have begun to write my book. I've written approximately _____ words of the manuscript.

▪ I consider the writing I've done on my book to be a very rough draft.

32 – Write Your Book! Publish Your Book! Market Your Book!

▪ I consider the writing I've done on my book to be fairly polished.

▪ I consider the writing I've done on my book to be a final version, needing beta readers and editing.

▪ What's a beta reader? (That question will be answered!)

Consider any of the above answers a triumph! A rough draft will become polished. A polished manuscript will become finalized. It's all systems go.

On, now, to the details involved in the transformation of your manuscript into your *BOOK!*

Editor, Proofreader

When you get to the point where you've completed your book, it's absolutely essential that you have proofreading, hopefully from several people, and not just a friend or family member. Include them, for sure, but I've seen time and again that different people notice different errors.

One person doesn't notice one kind of error, while another person spots it right off, or one reader is exceptionally good at spotlighting minor grammar boo-boos, when other people don't even know those lesser (yet still important!) grammar rules.

Your beta readers—the first people to read your completed book—are golden, if not more precious than gold. They catch typos, grammatical errors, inconsistencies in the text, holes in the plot, questions in the meaning, characters with unintentionally changing eye color like chameleons, and the like.

Your first readers are your champions, letting you know what they love in your book, and they also give you the bad news when something just isn't working.

One generally gathers beta readers slowly over time. A few people may come from friends and family, but most of them will be the people who have discovered your work, and love it.

They discover your work, perhaps from a giveaway you did through Amazon, Instafreebie, Goodreads, or with other writers, or solo, or they may have come upon your work on your own website or through your individual sales channel. My individual sales platform is Gumroad. More about Gumroad and other sales channels, in the ***Publish Your Book!*** section.

If you're fortunate enough to have amazing beta readers who are really good at editing as well as proofreading, you may not need to buy these services, which are not cheap. But be sure that you've given your book the very best attention you can give it. If you need professional editing, and/or proofreading, budget for it.

Because, as they say, you never have a second chance to make a first impression. And don't you want your book to be all it can be when you launch it?

> *"There is only one plot—
> things are not what they seem."*
> **Jim Thompson**

Pantsers Vs. Plotters

Let me engage in a bit of discussion regarding the ever-raging discourse among writers about "Pantsers vs. Plotters."

If you've been around writers at all of late, you've certainly heard this phrase, the subject being voiced with strong proponents on both sides. I too come down decidedly on one side of this fence, and that's on the side of plotting. But, for myself, I don't do too much.

The discussion goes something like this:

Pantsers say they don't plot, that plotting takes the surprise out of their writing, or stymies the flow of original language. (My apologies to any pantsers who feel that's an inadequate description—but I hope it captures the essence).

Plotters say—or what *I* say as a plotter—is that plotting at the outset of writing a book, and I mean anything from the sketchiest thumbnail sketch, to an elaborate, full-on outline, is the best way to see that a book gets written.

It helps more than tongue can tell when you're in the middle of the book asking yourself, "well, now what?" "How crazy am I?" "How did this ever seem like a good story/book idea?" And other self-castigating, abuse-heaping, comments to take the wind out of the sails of your creation.

It's not easy to write tens-of-thousands of words, juggling all the balls of creation it requires, holding in view each ever-rising mountain as the book progresses, maintaining the bird's-eye view of the overall book, while, at the same time, you're down in the gritty valleys of word-by-word creation.

An outline that chronicles the flow of your book is simply professional, in my opinion. Architects don't build buildings without a plan, a cake is not baked without a plan, college courses are carefully planned, a productive garden is planted and cared-for according to a plan.

Why would you give the blood, sweat, and tears of your life's work, your opus, any less attention?

> *When you write suspense,*
> *you have to know where you're going ...*
> *you have to drop little hints along the way.*
> *With the outline, I always know where the story is going.*
> *Before I ever write, I prepare an outline of 40 or 50 pages."*
> **John Grisham**

Here are some points of possible interest:

Most of the people I personally know who claim to be pantsers and who have produced many books, I suggest, are practiced at developing a plan in their minds early on, and, even if not committed to paper or computer, this is, in fact, an outline.

More relevant to the new writer, however, are the many writers who claim to be pantsers, *who have many partially-written books*. Say no more.

It's important to realize, too, that even if you write an outline, your book may change as you write. Your characters take over and begin to tell their true story. The story changes. If this happens, pause, have a chat with your characters to understand the new heading of your … ahem, *their* book, and produce at least a brief revised outline at the point where it departs from the previous plot line. A train runs on rails, and a book needs rails, as well.

A nonfiction book taking a dramatically new direction is less likely to occur, though it's possible. Some bit of research or interview may vastly inform you of your subject, and you need to refocus the overall trajectory of the book.

Honor your book. It cannot write itself (though sometimes, when you're in *flow,* it seems as though it does). If you don't have a map, the muddle in the middle can leave you lost in a wilderness of words that you may find yourself beginning to hate. Don't let that happen simply because of lack of planning.

Stories Have Structure

"Oh no," you cry. "Please, no more, just let me write."

Yes, we'll write, but first let's consider structure.

Returning to the scene of our ages-old story teller, why did rapt tribe members encircle the fire, night after night? What kept them coming back, rather than simply crawling into their cozy little twig and leaf beds?

They returned every evening as shades of night surrounded them, with curiosity and bated breath, because there was *structure* to the story telling. There was a familiar thread to the arc of the story, but there were also surprises. There were cliff-hangers.

A good story is a delicate dance between the familiar and the unknown.

There's plenty of bio-science about the way our brains are wired that has to do with survival. We need to be familiar with our environment, while, at the same time, we need the environment to present unknowns in order to learn how to be safe, even when the environment takes a turn into the unknown.

Simply put: we need to feel safe but we hate to be bored.

It's a dance….

There are a variety of excellent books for writers on story structure, but I'll stick to discussing one among my favorites, and that's Larry Brook's **Story Physics**.

Before becoming a convert to plotting, I'd struggle for months writing my books. The first time—with a degree of reluctance along with hopeful anticipation—I wrote a plan for my book, which was not a formal outline, but a musing of the book from beginning to end, it turned out to be about twelve pages, single spaced. I'll confess I was quite surprised that it was that long and that it flowed so readily. It came out all at once in about two-three hours—I subsequently wrote the book in six weeks.

I discovered that writing a book with my game plan in hand was great fun, I loved every minute of it. I didn't feel the least bit constrained by the story sketch. Instead, I felt greatly liberated.

When my protagonist took over the story and said, "no, you're wrong, court reporter, the story goes like this," I was delighted with the complexity and nuance that arose. It did so because I was in flow, and I was in flow because I had a solid but flexible knowledge of the story.

The story was able to become more complicated, more interesting, the characters gained depth, complexity, intrigue and charm, because I wasn't preoccupied with simply trying to know what the story was, trying to figure out what I'd write next.

I paused and listened to my characters, wrote the changes in the story line, then carried on.

I've continued since then to plot in the same manner for both my fiction and nonfiction books, and they all have been written in the framework of one to three months. *Whoo-hoo!* Feels awesome.

I could say more about the wonders of plotting, but let us cut to the chase as I share with you Larry Brooks' succinct particulars for story structure, which I've pared down, but present here enough for you to launch your plot line for your novel.

The points, less dramatically and more loosely translated, can be used to help define the flow of your nonfiction book, as well.

> *"Plot is ... footprints left in the snow after your characters have run by on their way to incredible destinations."*
> **Ray Bradbury**

I strongly recommend you buy Larry Brooks' book, *Story Physics*, to have his clarifying examples and details.

Larry Brooks – *Story Physics*:
There are, roughly, 60 scenes in a book.
Scenes 1-15, or 25 percent of the book, comprise *Part One*, the SETUP.

The SETUP shows what the protagonist has to lose, what's at stake. It engages the reader, and builds empathy with the character.

The following points are the attributes of *Part One*:
1. A grabber hook—at the outset there's tension and conflict, but the reader is unclear why. Your curious little fish reader is *hooked*.

2. You introduce the protagonist.
3. You pose what's at stake.
4. You weave in some foreshadowing.
5. You provide the "Inciting Incident"—something happens that propels the protagonist into the realm of the conflict of the story. *No turning back!*
6. You lay the groundwork for the First Plot Point.

The *First Plot Point* occurs around the first quarter of your book. Information and/or events enter the story, altering the protagonist's plan, beliefs, status, and actions. The *First Plot Point* defines the conflict the protagonist is now engaged in.

In the second quarter of the book, *Part Two*, Scenes 16-30, the protagonist responds, reacts, decides what to do, or is fraught with indecision about the information posed by the dilemma of the *Inciting Incident* and the *First Plot Point*.

A new quest is formed by the raised stakes.

At the halfway point of the book, moving from *Part Two* to *Part Three*, new information enters the story that motivates the protagonist to move into a "warrior" position, anything from, in a small, quiet story, actively attempting to fix things, to, in larger stories, becoming an actual, active warrior.

The protagonist realizes, in *Part Three*, Scenes 31-45, that personal growth and change, as well as solving the external problem, is part of what's required to triumph. Near the middle of the third section, there arises the "All Hope is Lost" quandary.

The *Second Plot Point* comes at the three-quarter point of the book. This is an important moment when the last new information enters the story. After this point, *no new information about the problem or challenge may be introduced* (new information after this point feels extremely contrived, and *does not work*).

This new information is the last piece of the puzzle, and within this framework, the protagonist is given everything needed to become the catalyst, the hero or heroine, in the story's conclusion.

In *Part Four*, Scenes 46-60, there is resolution. The protagonist employs all the resources, wisdom, supporters, and tools that have been presented to bring the story home to its fulfilled conclusion, whether happy or sad.

The protagonist is willing to die, either literally or figuratively, to cause good—or what the protagonist deems as good—to prevail. As the climax mounts and the denouement is resolved, the reader, laughing or crying, is with the protagonist to the end, whether the protagonist succeeds, or, in darker work, fails.

Larry Brooks provides a beautiful, *beautiful* exposition of the book **The Help**, showing how perfectly it aligns with his articulation of the arc of story telling. Just in case you felt the plan only applies to expansive science fiction, fantasy or techno-thriller novels, it's just as meaningfully applied to smaller, real world, literary works.

Now, if you have a visceral and unpleasant reaction to the "formality" of the foregoing approach to writing a book, I imagine you are, at core, a pantser. But I remain steadfast in the recommendation that you write at least an informal story or nonfiction book arc, and give thought to it hitting the above-mentioned points.

I cannot emphasize enough how much the future you, when you're at thirty- or forty-thousand words, will either be grateful that you engaged this advice … or wish you had.

*"Nothing stinks
like a pile of unpublished writing."*
Sylvia Plath

Publish Your Book!

Where to start? Getting published is a big can 'o worms—it seems that everything must be done at the same time, which is sort of true, but, since it's impossible to do everything at the same time, we'll consider the various pieces of the puzzle, one at a time.

Your Website

You must have a website, and, of course, you'll have to have a domain name, preferably your own name. If you name is extremely common, or maybe even not so very common, but still, someone has taken it, come up with the next best options. Add your middle name, or otherwise brainstorm and search domain names until you come up with one that is distinctly you. Grab it quick before it goes. You will do this through your web host. So that leads to….

You need web hosting. I'm with *Bluehost* – *http://bit.ly/hostblu* and have been since the dawn of time. No host is perfect, and *Bluehost* fits that category, but, they are available to talk with 24-7, in U.S. Mountain Time Zone.

Sometimes they answer right away, and sometimes one is on hold for a lengthy wait.

But most of the tech help is bright, patient, and helpful. There are a couple people who are not—you'll know them if you get them. There's a quality control survey at the end of the call, which I recommend people take advantage of, if service was particularly good or particularly bad.

Wordpress

Yay! You have your hosting and your domain name. Now you need a website. This is where the wonder of Wordpress enters the scene. I'm giving you only a tiny sketch of what to do, as there are numerous resources, including YouTube tutorials, about how to access and build your website via *Wordpress.org* (you want to host your own domain, and thus will need to go through *Wordpress.org* to set it up).

First, you'll choose a Wordpress theme to work with, and then you'll learn how to build your website. I appreciate that it may seem daunting, but if you take it baby-step-by-baby-step, you'll soon discover that you've built a website! All by yourself!

If you don't want to build a website, all by yourself, there are a plethora of services that will put up a site for you. However, I *strongly recommend* you do this relatively easy work yourself, for the pragmatic reason that you will want to be able to add, change, correct, remove pages, posts, or change your layout, so on and so forth *yourself*, as needed, at any moment.

In addition, I've heard horror story after horror story of people who had a service build their website in some a-typical way, then the service dematerialized and the site owners could not get back into their own website.

A word to the wise: the best thing you can learn at this moment is how to build a simple Wordpress site. Unless you happen to have someone in your life who does this sort of thing, then … lucky you!

Now Then....

You have a domain, you have hosting, you have a barebones, but lovely, website. You have a book.

How to orchestrate it all? The tympani are rumbling around, the flutes don't know what they're doing, and the first violinist is tearing out his hair, wondering where the conductor is.

You enter the theatre. You will make music of it all. Your book is in Scrivener. You raise your baton and, with a downbeat, you call upon *FILE* in Scrivener. Making sure that all the components are in place, you command *COMPILE*. The music begins.

In a few seconds, you have a gorgeous epub. Kobo will upload this epub, iBooks will upload this epub, Nook will upload this epub, and, yes, thrilled audience, even Amazon is now able to make a beautiful book out of your epub.

You can also compile a .mobi, Amazon's native file format, or a PDF, which you can export to .doc to download into CreateSpace, or take into InDesign to format beautifully, if you have InDesign, for your print book.

WOW! Fantastic!

You will now need to look at your new epub. I do this with the iBooks software:
iTunes Producer – bookcreator.com/2013/11/publish-itunes-step-2-install-itunes-producer
which you can download for free after you register with iBooks, if you haven't already. Fast and tidy.

And then, yes, when your book is a beautiful epub, it's likely you will see boo-boos and errors, and things you just don't like about the look of your epub.

No problem! You go into your book file in Scrivener, fix the errors, improve the text, change the layout, whatever it needs, and click File > Compile again. It's not unusual for me to do this a dozen times before I'm satisfied with my book. I tend to have complicated layouts, so it will likely be less challenging for you.

And then, the great moment you've looked forward to—the moment you upload your very own book onto the publishing platforms of your choice. Is it not wondrous to be able to do this with your book? You, yourself, single-handedly, are now publishing your work!

Your Cover

However! You don't have a book until you have a cover. I can attest to the importance of a cover by the robust sales of one of my nonfiction books in a series, against the less stellar sales of another book in the series. To me, the covers are not that different, but, clearly they are different to the buying public, with the one book out-selling the other five-to-one.

I have the advantage of being a graphic artist, and have worked with Photoshop and InDesign since their beginnings, years ago. I produce all my own covers, as well as those of a couple other folks on occasion. But, if you don't happen to have graphic art and production skills, as everyone says, you will need to pay for a good cover.

If you *do* have a graphic arts background and intend to produce your own covers, there are several websites that offer totally free, royalty free images. My favorite is *Pixabay.com*, and there are others as well. But be sure to check that any free image you intend to use is royalty free and in the public domain, which you can confirm via Creative Commons, *creativecommons.org*. There are, of course, paid image services such as Getty Images and Shutterstock.

There is a *very* wide range of cover artists, with an equally wide range of fees. Here's a link to a page of book cover artists compiled by BookBub. Since I've not used any cover artists, my thanks to BookBub.com for this list, which includes examples of the covers of each service: *https://insights.bookbub.com/fantastic-book-cover-design-resources/*

As always, *caveat emptor*. Carefully vet and research anyone, any service, any app, any software, you consider employing.

> *"I try to keep it simple:*
> *Tell the damned story."*
> **Tom Clancy**

A Word (Okay, a Bunch of Words) About ISBNs

Your ISBN—International Standardized Book Number—on your book is a number provided, in the U.S., by Bowker.com. Individual countries have their own ISBN agency.

Several of the foregoing publishing sites (Amazon, iBooks, Kobo, Nook, Draft2Digital) will provide you with an ISBN, free of charge, which is a great advantage, but the downside is, they list themselves as the publisher. If you intend to have your own imprint/publisher name, and become established with that name—which I strongly recommend—you'll need your own ISBN.

In some countries, for example, Canada, ISBNs are free. But in the U.S. and England and some other countries, they are quite expensive. As of this writing, ISBNs are $125 for one, $295 for ten, $595 for 100, and considerably less for larger numbers of ISBNs, from Bowker in the U.S. And the prices occasionally go up.

The prices of the ISBNs reflect Bowker's clear preference for publishers building a catalog over the individual author, which, in my opinion, is simply *wrong*. But please give the whole ISBN matter serious thought. If the only way you can publish as you start out is to avail yourself of free ISBNs, then do so. It *is* an advantage to be given an ISBN, but consider it a temporary fix. As soon as you can, get your own ISBNs, and reload your books to the various sites with *your* ISBNs and *your* publishing imprint.

Keep in mind that all the while your book is on the various sites with all the different ISBNs, your book is not getting the traction it would with your imprint's one, exclusive, ISBN. The entire ISBN muddle has made a mess of the intention of the ISBN, which is, as its name attempts to imply, an International *Standardized* Book Number.

That is to say, the intention and the significance of the system is that a book has but one ISBN, from its publishing entity, whether an individual or a huge publisher. This number appends to the title, making the book "findable" by that one number in databases around the world.

But, as you can see, if your book has an ISBN from Amazon, another from iBooks, another from Nook, another from Kobo, so on and so forth, the ISBN's intended function and purpose has been lost. All of the bookstores will let you list your book with *your own* ISBN, and none of them will let you use an ISBN from another store on their site.

Further, you may come upon "bargain basement" ISBNs from other entities on the internet. Do not, repeat, *DO NOT* buy these numbers. They are not usable. They are either recycled, or in some way black market. When you look up your book under "your" ISBN that you inexpensively bought, you'll see that your imprint is not attached to your book.

Even worse, when you're ready to upload your book with these "not real" ISBNs at Ingram, for instance, they will not take on your books for distribution, because the number is shown as already in use by another company, publisher, or imprint, *not yours*. And so, in order to distribute your book with the world's largest book distributor, you'll end up having to buy an ISBN from Bowker.

Best practice is simply to buy as many ISBNs as you can afford for the number of books you imagine publishing. If you're in a country that understands publishing must not be impinged upon by an inappropriate fee for an identifying number, then lucky you!

Off to Amazon!

Now, you're ready for Amazon. First, you'll establish your account on Kindle Direct Publishing – *kdp.amazon.com*. Then—at last!—you'll be face to face with your empty virtual bookshelf, humming with anticipation for your book/s!

Follow the simple 1, 2, 3, directions to upload your book, filling in all the fields, and giving concerted attention to writing interesting, "grabbing" copy for your book's detail page.

If you feel your copy is weak, and you're challenged to write a succinct, compelling, dynamic blurb, consider paying for this service. It's not easy to condense, distill, and serve up the essence, like clarified ghee, of your entire work in just a few words. Ask any author!

To help you do this, read what authors of successful books in your niche, or nearby categories, write (or pay to have written) about their high-ranking book on their book's detail page, and emulate them.

Do not copy, that's a no-no. But wrap your mind around the language, the pacing of the language, the length of the text (this can vary from book to book, and genre to genre, but, once again, I suggest taking up the available space with compelling text), and any other point you observe on the detail pages of successful books that strikes you as relevant to the cause at hand—which is, your book, ranking well and selling, right out of the gate.

To recap: your book blurb and your cover are your *most important* marketing pieces. Think of it as part of your job description as publisher to assure that these vital components of your book are attractive, engaging, and **STRONG**.

> *"Writers live twice."*
> **Natalie Goldberg**

Your Author Page on Amazon

Be sure to claim your Amazon Author Page. This additional "virtual real estate" is where you can put a photograph of yourself, a bit of bio, commentary on your books, photos, or video, a feed of your blog, and info about upcoming events, such as book launches or book signings.

There's quite a bit of leeway here—you can do all of the foregoing, or very little of it. You can even put a picture of your cat if you prefer, but I advise you to let your readers know who you are. If they've gone out of their way to visit your Amazon Author page, they really want to know about *YOU*—that's so cool! So give them what they're looking for. *https://authorcentral.amazon.com*

CreateSpace – Amazon

CreateSpace is awesome – *https://www.createspace.com/*. The books produced are beautiful, the team is knowledgeable and pleasant, easy to reach by email or phone, and they really go the distance to support you, being helpful in any way they can.

I'm extremely impressed with the CreateSpace product. My book, Life Flows on the River of Love – *bit.ly/gumroadlifeflows* is a full color, full bleed (the images go to the very edge on every page), 8.5" x 11" poster-like book (not exactly a poster book, as pages are printed on both sides).

I was trepidatious when I received the box from CreateSpace containing the first copies. How had the images turned out? They looked great printed out from my printer and on the computer screen. But here was my fussy book, that I spent many hours producing, about to be revealed.

I was stunned. Some of the images are even more impressive than those printed on my expensive printer. Some of the pages have a gorgeous, metallic, coppery cast. Yes. Stunned, I was.

People say CreateSpace product matches books printed by big publishers. I say CreateSpace books often excel books printed by big publishers. And further, you cannot beat CreateSpace's attention to authors. When, a couple years ago, I got books with a defect, I called them, and new books were sent to me directly, no cost, no argument.

Kobo

Kobo's author site is *https://www.kobo.com/writinglife*. The site is stream-lined, it's easy to put up your books, and Kobo has, all in all, a "classier" feel/presence than Amazon. Amazon is for the masses, which is fine, no complaints about that fact, while Kobo is a bit more refined.

An advantage of Kobo over Amazon is that it pays authors 70 percent on their books, no matter the book's price, no matter where sold, whereas Amazon pays only 35 percent below $2.99 and above $9.99, with the 70 percent only applying from $2.99-$9.99, and that only in the major markets (i.e., 35 percent in Brazil, Japan, and other markets, unless you've opted to be exclusive with Amazon, and have enrolled in KDP Select). Now, if only Kobo could get the sales Amazon has!

iBooks

You'll set up and access your iBooks account through iTunes producer:
bookcreator.com/2013/11/publish-itunes-step-2-install-itunes-producer/

It's not the easiest system to work with, and, as much as I anticipated iBooks to really perform, in my experience, it has not. I hope your experience is considerably more positive. You might want to have an aggregator (discussed further on) place your books on the iBooks platform, saving you precious time, which you can devote to writing your next book.

Nook

Ah! the poor, beleaguered, Barnes & Noble Nook – *www.nookpress.com*. Yes, some of my books are on B&N Nook. No, I see virtually no return on them. Yes, hope springs eternal. It's mystifying to me and other indie authors why Barnes & Noble worked so hard to kill a perfectly decent product and system.

The Nook's assistance for authors began at non-existent and rose all the way to egregious. I say *was*, because I haven't tried to communicate with them in years. The last I did, I was treated with overt rudeness. My goodness!

Barnes & Noble seems, recently, to be trying to raise the Phoenix from the ashes, but the attempt seems weak, and other authors and myself remain mystified by their sadly ineffective efforts.

News Flash: It seems that Barnes & Noble is "waving the white flag" of defeat regarding the Nook, with speculation that B&N might sell what remains of the Nook universe to Kobo, as noted by Bryan Cohen on the *Sell More Books*

Podcast. A logical move, and good for what's left of Nook, but sad to lose a major contender from the field of competition, even if it had weak performance.

Ingram Spark/Lightning Source

Ingram is the largest physical book distributor in the world. Ingram/LS – *https://www.ingramcontent.com/publishers/lp/lightning-source*. They charge a fee to upload your book, and they charge a fee to upload corrections, which I truly do not understand, because, as they're the largest book distributor in the world, wouldn't they want the product they distribute to be as perfect as possible, and not charge $25 to make any correction?

For myself, I'm producing many books, and I want each new book to be noted on my book list in every previous book, so I'd, ideally, make corrections to all my books on a fairly regular basis. No one else charges a fee to re-upload books, so it's doubly weird that Ingram does.

Your books in Ingram's system means that they are available in bookstores all around the world, Barnes & Noble, Waterstones, etc., etc., as well as in the data base of university libraries and public libraries. It's exciting, I must say. Ingram Spark/Lightning Source also produces hardbound books.

Think about it, your book, *hardbound*. Expensive, but oh-so-gorgeous!

Wattpad

Wattpad.com is a free online storytelling community. Users post stories, fan-fic, novels-in-progress, poetry, articles, etc. Anyone can comment on and "like" content. A number of writers have discovered success on Wattpad. For example, Hugh Howey's *Wool* started out on Wattpad.

Many authors have been cautious about putting their work up on Wattpad, as it's a form of publication and is no longer exclusive. But times have changed, and now agents and editors comb Wattpad and other sites for promising work.

Wattpad is a platform where you can receive valuable feedback and gather followers who love your work. And, extra possible bonus, you may be offered a publishing contract, which you can choose to accept or refuse.

Aggregators

Aggregators publish books to the various sites, freeing you, the writer, to write more books, while the aggregator takes care of sales, for a nominal fee.

The aggregator that has been around the longest and is perhaps familiar to you is Smashwords. While Smashwords is still running strong, there are a number of other aggregators who have come on the scene over the years, with differing advantages, but all of the ones I list here provide, to the best of my knowledge, good-to-great service for reasonable fees.

Let's take a brief look at a few of them ….

Smashwords

Smashwords.com is the brainchild of Mark Coker, brilliant and well-liked by everyone, who, early on, worked to give Amazon a run for its money. Smashwords is not, perhaps, as popular as it initially was, mostly, I believe, for not developing the manuscript-translating software so that it's easier to use. But it's still a strong contender, and there's no denying that Mr. Coker has defended and championed indies every step of the way.

Smashwords aggregates and distributes to:

iBooks

Barnes & Noble (Nook)

Kobo

Baker & Taylor – Baker-Taylor.com – US book distributors for over 180 years.

Gardners.com – The United Kingdom's largest book wholesaler.

Scribd.com – a subscription service

Overdrive.com – One of the most significant library platforms.

Draft2Digital

Oh, yay, Draft2Digital (*https://www.draft2digital.com/*). They turn your manuscript into an epub, or whatever form the publisher needs, and sends it out, at present count, to the following sites:

iBooks

Barnes & Noble (Nook)

Kobo

Inktera.com – Book seller

Playster.com – a subscription site with a few problems, the major one being that a number of authors have complained that they are listing their pirated books

Scribd.com – a subscription site

24symbols.com – Based in Madrid, Spain, 24 Symbols is an ebook subscription service with a catalog of thousands of books in more than ten languages

Tolino.com – German ebook alliance of leading German booksellers, with fifteen-hundred bookstores across Germany. Excellent!

Overdrive.com – One of the most significant library platforms

FindawayVoices.com – a relatively new audiobooks distributor

You can make your life easier by having Draft2Digital do the work of getting your book/s on any or all of those sites according to your preference. (You will notice the absence of Amazon, as Amazon does not work with D2D.)

In exchange for approximately 10–15 percent of your book sales, you have the freedom of time to write more books—which have the potential of producing more than that 10-15 percent, does it not? In addition, Draft2Digital's broad footprint likely contributes to generating sales, I suspect, more than distributing solely on one's own.

Another outstanding advantage of Draft2Digital is their Books2Read.com site. Here you can make a universal book link for your book that will take your reader to every site where your book appears. This is a huge plus!

For example, the universal book link will automatically take potential customers to the Amazon site in their country. Without the universal book link, you would have to list each Amazon site, and every other store site, individually. Not only is this a massive task, but impossibly clutters your book's promotion.

They also have a free landing page option, with the book's cover and description, along with the universal book link. You can link to and from your website or social media post to these landing pages. *WOW!*

Draft2Digital makes a PDF for your print book for free, offers an automatic submission to Goodreads and other catalog sites option, and an automatic "new release" option. You can create a pen name under your publisher account if you so desire, and you can create a sales page.

Publish Drive

Publishdrive.com is a Hungarian aggregator that distributes to over four-hundred stores, in excess of one-hundred countries, and to numerous libraries, including libraries in China and India. They charge a flat 10 percent of the net sale.

This seems like a notable venue for getting into some potentially exciting, otherwise inaccessible, markets.

> *"I don't care if a reader hates one of my stories, just as long as he finishes the book."*
> — *Roald Dahl*

Subscription Services

Amazon's Kindle Unlimited – KU

Let me share with you some thoughts about Amazon's subscription service, Kindle Unlimited, and, while I'm at it, Kindle Direct Publishing (KDP). Details on both can be found at kdp.amazon.com. The following is my subjective opinion, arising from personal experience.

There is a significant population of authors in KU, who are pleased with it, and who are making enough money to determine that the relationship is viable for them. However, I've removed almost all my books and stories from KDP Select and Kindle Unlimited as I've simply not seen performance in these programs that is adequate to agree to exclusivity.

Like many authors, I don't care for the slash-and-burn automation of the bots that authors must accept on Amazon's platform. Though I continue to play on Amazon's playground, I believe it's important, and, in fact, *professional*, to have my work available via the rich variety of other sites.

At the same time, I laud and compliment the people who work in Author Central, Create Space, and Kindle Direct

Publishing. I've talked with many of them, and 99.9 percent of them are patient, sincere, hard-working, and really, truly, mean to help authors.

The problem, however, is the vast amount of basic information they don't have. For one small instance, I very recently voiced my oft-repeated complaint regarding Amazon regularly taking down book reviews (mine and other authors). The Amazon employee I was talking with was absolutely stunned, and insightfully asked, "why would they do that? Why? Don't the reviews belong to the book? Don't the reviews help sell the book?"

He had no idea that Amazon took down book reviews. This was a person in a town, as it happens, a few miles from me, in my same time zone, which is the same as Amazon in Seattle. In other words, we're all in Washington state. So—even a person physically close to Amazon, who works for Amazon, who works with writers, did not know that Amazon regularly takes down book reviews.

He asked why reviews are regularly taken down. Yes. Why? These bright and kind employees are not aware of many other aspects of Amazon's handling of authors. When stumped, which is frequent, they reply with the only thing they *can* reply, which is, "it's the bots."

Therefore, I advise against the "all eggs in a single basket" concept of KDP Select and KU. If you opt to become exclusive, may your experience be positive and lucrative. But please pay close attention to the steward, clarifying the exit path.

Playster and Scribd

I feel doubtful about subscription services such as Playster.com and Scribd.com, as there are too uncomfortably many accusations of copyright infringement. Do your research!

Many authors, including myself, are altogether not fond of the subscription model—either buy a book or don't, or, conversely, borrow it from your local library. But there are numerous subscription services, and there'll be more, so authors must determine if this is a viable model for their work, or not.

> *"Do not hoard what seems good*
> *for a later place in the book,*
> *or for another book; give it,*
> *give it all, give it now."*
> **Annie Dillard**

A Storefront of Your Own

Gumroad

How about having your own store, your books, your audio books, other products if you make other things, in your own store? There are several options to choose from. I like and use Gumroad, *gumroad.com*. I like the fun, friendly interface. It's so, *so* super-duper easy to put up your product, in all formats.

Gumroad provides easy drag and drop creation of unlimited listings. The fees range from a free account, with transaction fees at 8.5 percent plus 30 cents per transaction, to $10 per month for fewer than one-thousand customers, up to $250 per month for over fifty-thousand customers, with a transaction fee of 3.5 percent plus 30 cents per transaction.

Gumroad also has a free newsletter tool, plus you can share and sell your products on social media, blogs, or email with product links.

Books can be made available in epub, mobi, and PDF. Gumroad also watermarks the PDF, so that if a buyer treats it like something they feel they need to pirate, the author is apprised of the fact. I'm in the process of building my Gumroad site, which you can visit to see a simple and easy-to-create store: *https://gumroad.com/Blythe*

Selz

Selz.com is another popular storefront for authors. Their store options range from $0 per month with a limit of 5 items with a 2 percent transaction fee and a 2.9 percent plus 30 cents processing fee, to $12.99 per month with unlimited items, a 2 percent transaction fee and a 2.9 percent plus 30 cents processing fee, to a $26.99 months fee, unlimited items, no transaction fee and the same 2.9 percent plus 30 cents processing fee.

Shopify

Shopify.com starts at $29 per month, with a transaction fee of 2.9 percent plus 30 cents.

Storenvy

You can build your own, individual storefront at Storenvy.com, and you can also have your listings in their marketplace, where people can readily find your ebooks, and other products, if you have them, all for free. Storenvy takes 10 percent for sales in the Storenvy Marketplace, while the revenue from the sales on your own Storenvy site is all yours (less transaction fees).

As I peruse the books on Storenvy, I see it's strong on nonfiction and illustrated books, not so strong for novels. Let's change that—it's a great site, with a good payout system. You may note the high number of negative reviews, but they are for individual sellers, not Storenvy itself, which is generally liked.

Facebook Pages

Yes, you can have a store on Facebook.com. After making a Facebook page for your brand, you click the "shop" tab, fill in the required information, then build your shop, free and easy to run from right inside Facebook. Standard processing fees apply.

eBay

Another, perhaps somewhat strange-sounding place to sell your books, is on eBay.com. Although I've not done this yet, given how many listings there are for my books on eBay, it seems like authors ought to have their own listings there, also. I'm a bit bemused by so much presence of my books on eBay, but I imagine, as listings are free until there's a sale, there are people who put up bunches of books, in the hopes of making a sale.

Unless my books on eBay are pirated, it's all the same to me. If there's a sale, it will go through CreateSpace for a physical book, or KDP for an ebook (or any of the other vendors where my books are sold, if that's the channel the seller operates through, for example, Rakutan for my Kobo ebooks, or Ingram for my physical books), and I make the same money as with any other sale. So, in concept, I'm perfectly happy to see my books on eBay via other sellers.

Your Own Website

You can get into ecommerce and build a store on your own website. The details are beyond the scope of this book, so I'll just mention it, and you can begin to consider the option.

The particular advantage of an ecommerce store on your website is that you can put direct links from your website to both your ebooks and your physical books on Amazon, Ingram, iBooks, Kobo, and other sites.

You can also have physical books on hand, and mail the copies you sell. Not a project I care for, but it *is* an option.

Of course you'll make the most money from your ebooks if you have them downloadable on your own site. But keep in mind that you'll have to address and solve what has gone wrong when there are problems.

When you link to other platforms (Gumroad, Amazon, iBooks, Kobo, etc.), via your website's ecommerce store, you'll make a bit less than having them downloadable on your site, but you'll have fewer headaches.

I strongly recommend having your own store front, whether on your website or on a store platform, where you have control and autonomy.

Amazon is continually changing, and other platforms change, too. Make a footprint, no matter how small it is at first. At least it's *your* footprint. It will grow if you give it attention. And it'll be there if things change beyond your comfort zone on any of the other platforms.

> *"The best self promotion is your next book.*
> *And the book after that and after that ..."*
> **Bella Andre**

Audiobooks

Audiobooks are coming full-force upon the scene, with many authors seeing a notable boost in their audio sales. Here's a thumbnail sketch of a few of the major players in audio book production and distribution:

ACX

ACX.com distributes audiobooks to Audible, an Amazon company, and iTunes. If your already-produced audiobook meets their specs, they will publish it to those powerful selling platforms.

Or, if your prefer, ACX has available the resources and talent to produce your book. You can choose from a variety of narrator talent. The amount of money you make from the sales of your audiobook depends on the agreement you arrive at—whether you decide to distribute wide, or to be exclusive with ACX, and if you have a royalty split with your narrator and producer.

Check out ACX for the particulars of these various options, and be sure to look into their generous bounty program.

Audible
Audible.com, as noted, is Amazon's audio book company.

iBooks
Your ACX produced audiobook can be distributed to Apple's iBooks. Although it appears to download via iTunes, it will play in iBooks.

Findaway Voices
Finally! Some strong competition for ACX. If you access findawayvoices.com through draft2digital.com, they will waive their $49.00 service fee. When your book is produced through Findaway Voices, or you produce it yourself and upload it via D2D, you will reach more than 170 countries by the world's leading audiobook distribution network.

You will have complete control of your audiobook's content, pricing, and distribution, along with access to professional narrators. If you choose not to narrate your book yourself, you'll be guided through production, and end up with a quality product, ready for any audiobook platform.

ListenUp
Listenupindie.pub provides complete audiobook production and distribution. They distribute to:

Audible

iTunes

Downpour.com – an audiobook club

Barnes & Noble

Scribd

Audiobooks.com

Libro.fm, which distributes to bookstores
And to the following sites, which all distribute to libraries:

OverDrive

Bibliotheca

Baker & Taylor

Follett Library Services

Macklin Educational

HOOPLA – hoopladigital.com

ListenUp also uploads your audiobook to their own platform, Listenupindie.pub

You can opt into or out of any of the platforms.

Payment is 80 percent of the amount ListenUp receives, which sounds great until you realize that from Audible, ListenUp receives only 25 percent of the list price, and the author gets 80 percent of 25 percent. But you'll receive the full 80 percent with any sales from the ListenUp platform.

I'm unclear as to where the narrator and producer's money comes from, if you don't self-produce.

Author's Republic

Authorsrepublic.com is very similar to ListenUp, except the author receives 70 percent of what the audio book earns. The have distribution to 30 channels, with a list that looks quite similar to ListenUp.

Kobo

Kobo.com has recently announced that they are distributing audiobooks. *This is great news!*

> *"Writing saved me from the sin and inconvenience of violence."*
> *Alice Walker*

Help Getting Published

And yet more publication goodies. Here is a very short list of editors, proofreaders, cover artists, and other helping-type people and sites.

Editors & Proofreaders

inkspokes.com/resource-links/editors-proofreaders– Children's publishing – all things kid-lit.

www.bookdocs.com – The Independent Editors Group

www.bookworks.com – The Self-Publishers Association

www.bibliocrunch.com – Bibliocrunch

www.consulting-editors.com – Consulting Editors Alliance
www.digitalbookworld.com – Digital Book World

www.upwork.com – Offering a variety of assistants, virtual assistants (VAs), sales and marketing experts, accountants, mobile developers, designers, web development, etc.

www.the-efa.org – Editorial Freelancers Association

www.mediabistro.com – Media Bistro

www.publishersmarketplace.com – Publishers Market Place

www.fundsforwriters.com/freelance-editors-for-indie-authors – freelance editors for indie authors.

Joanna Penn's site: for a trust worthy list of professional author-helpers – www.thecreativepenn.com/editors

Cover Artists
Thank you Bookbub for providing this list – insights.bookbub.com/fantastic-book-cover-design-resources

Virtual Assistants
fiverr: https://www.fiverr.com – for five dollars, or more, you can get a book cover, editorial assistants, and other vir-

tual assistants. Some wonderful connections here, some, not so much. *Caveat emptor!*

There are numerous sources of VAs, virtual assistants, in various places in the world, with a significant number of VA businesses in the Philippines. Do a Google search, and do your due diligence if engaging any virtual assistant. I'd be interested in hearing about your experience if you hire a VA, what the experience is like, good and not so good, that I can share with others.

The Alliance of Independent Authors - ALLi

ALLi – The Alliance of Independent Authors – allianceindependentauthors.org is an organization that champions, supports, and defends the indie author and indie movement. An Irish lass by the name of Orna Ross is at the helm. She's a brilliant, action-taking, action-making author, leading the vanguard of indie success.

ALLi vets an extensive range of services including editors, graphic artists, marketing experts, and others, who are fully apprised of indie author needs.

ALLi also leads several significant campaigns. A couple of them are ALLi's watchdog campaign, to assure that indie authors do not get "taken" by less than scrupulous businesses that prey on authors, and an "Open Up to Indie Authors" Campaign to encourage literary festivals, events, prizes, reviewers, and booksellers to include indie authors.

They also have a series of guidebooks for authors, which are free to members.

My favorite activity of ALLi's is the Indie Author Fringe, ALLi's three times a year online self-publishing conference. Slam-jam-packed with info from indie authors who walk their talk, and who generously share their knowledge, experience, and insights. It's free for everyone, and because of that, as well as some other perks, I became a member.

Watching Out for Writers:
Science Fiction Writers of America – SFWA
sfwa.org, is a Professional Science Fiction/Fantasy organization.

SFWA's Writer Beware: On the SFWA site, look under "Resources" then, "Writer Beware." This is current and relevant information about unethical agents, editors, publishers, designers, and others working in the book industry. SFWA's Writer Beware is relevant for all authors, not only SF/F authors. Check it out regularly.

Written Word Media
writtenwordmedia.com – Somewhat similar to SFWA's Writer Beware

Absolute Write
Absolute Write – Water Cooler Forums – Also somewhat similar to SFWA's Writer Beware.

Kboards
Kboards – kboards.com – An endless fount of author info too vast to even attempt to describe here. You must simply check it out for yourself.

The Alliance of Independent Authors
ALLi – allianceindependentauthors.org – see above.

The Hot Sheet
The Hot Sheet – hotsheetpub.com – $50 annually. When you get to a full-time writerly career, and even before, Jane Friedman and Porter Anderson's Hot Sheet is a time saving plethora of up-to-the-minute information.

Just for the fun of it….
Here are a few other online stores (there are gazillions, more or less), not book-related, but great for arts and other things, if you happen to be an artist, photographer, or maker of other awesome delights:

Cart66:	cart66.com
Society6:	society6.com
Zazzle:	zazzle.com
Fine Art America:	fineartamerica.com
Redbubble:	redbubble.com
Deviant Art:	deviantart.com

"You may delay, but time will not."
Benjamin Franklin

Market Your Book!

Now that you've accomplished all the wonderful and amazing goals of writing your book, having your book edited and proofread, getting the book formatted for an ebook and a physical book, getting a stellar cover made for it, deciding if you'll have an audiobook and if you'll record it or have it recorded, getting your book up on many of the book-selling sites—you can sit back and relax, right?

No my dear peer writer friend, all of the previous work is the behind-the-stage groundwork, for the "great reveal" of your work via *marketing*.

Your List

You'll hear frequent discussions among indie authors about *"The List."* Your list is composed of the people who have signed up to learn more about what you write. When you send emails—your newsletter—to your list (not *too* frequently), make them fascinating, and relevant to what your readers are anticipating.

Instafreebie

There are a variety of ways to get people onto your list. The first one I'll address here is Instafreebie.com.

Instafreebie is a site that offers free downloaded stories, novels, nonfiction books and partials to its followers, in exchange for their email on the list of the author whose work they've just downloaded. The results for some authors has been quite impressive, netting them hundreds and even thousands of followers added to their email list, and generating a boost in sales of other books in an author's series.

Further, genre-specific Instafreebie authors do group giveaways, pooling their lists, which is a win-win for both reader and authors, as readers may get as many as forty free books, stories, or partials in their favorite genre/s, and the authors share their lists with one another. Instafreebie has initiated a couple of new programs that promise to stimulate its productivity, which will be fantastic.

Check out Instafreebie and see for yourself what it might have to offer you, as a writer *and* as a reader.

Bookfunnel

Bookfunnel.com is an ebook delivery app to assure that your books get to your beta readers, that ARCs (Advanced Reader's Copies), are delivered, and that copies of your books are sent to anyone you want to send them to, regardless of what sort of device the recipient may read on, or if they want your book sent via email to put on their desktop.

Seamless and no hassle, this book delivery system frees you to write, rather than trying to solve delivery problems. Bookfunnel plans range from $20 per year for one author name and five thousand downloads per month, to $250 per year for three author names and unlimited downloads, as well as several other features.

Your Email Service

Once you have an email list, you'll want to communicate with the people on it. There are a number of email services, but the two I'll discuss here are the ones I have direct experience with:
MailChimp – *MailChimp.com*
MailerLite – *MailerLite.com*

Both of these services have very reasonable fees, as well as significant free parameters, including free landing pages, and numerous useful services as your list grows.

MailChimp has been around for a long time, while Mailerlite, in Finland—or is it Latvia?, their info is ambiguous—is a rather new kid on the block, relatively speaking. But it has put the challenge to other email services.

MailChimp's documentation gets regular complaints for its obtuse instructions and, even worse, unavailability of any help, whatsoever, by a human for a free account. Those two factors put a damper on my wanting to grow my relationship with MailChimp into a paid account. If a business won't let me interact with their customer service before purchase, I'm much less likely to engage in their paid service.

I need to have an idea of how good their customer and tech services are. Don't you?

However, Mailchimp does have a two-thousand free list maximum, whereas Mailerlite's maximum list before (a modest) payment, is one-thousand. On another hand, as of this writing, each increment of their paid levels is less than MailChimp's, and, ultimately, less expensive.

But, oh my goodness, Mailerlite's attention to customers and potential customers is stellar. While still considering if I would sign on to Mailerlite and more or less undo everything I've done in MailChimp—*which is a lot of work!*—I emailed Mailerlite with a couple questions. They answered me directly and personally and with amazing thoroughness. Five stars, plus, plus. *****++!

Then I had more questions as I employed their service, and engaged in the best online chat I've ever had with any business service—more powerful, more available, more personable.

In addition, they have free landing pages that you can easily build for your books. MailChimp has now followed suit, seeing the competition, and, I suppose, watching clients and potential clients move to Mailerlite's platform.

Give them both a trial run, and see how they fit your needs. Also, you can use them both, if you want to get creative, up to their free maximum and save some money until your list(s) grow beyond three-thousand.

Other email services authors use: ConvertKit.com, ActiveCampaign.com, AWeber.com, InfusionSoft.com, ConstantContact.com, GetResponse.com, SendinBlue.com. There are others, but I believe these are the ones with the most author involvement.

What to Do with Your List?

Your email list is your gold mine. It's made up of the people specifically interested in your work, who have given you a valued bit of themselves—their email address. Your assignment, should you choose to accept it, is to *keep* them interested in your work. Write the books they look forward to getting, send them emails/newsletters they open and read.

How often, and what the emails contain, is entirely up to you. Some authors are rather formal in their newsletters, and don't send them very often, while other authors are chatty and communicate frequently. And all points in-between. You'll learn by doing.

One thing for sure, never have your communication with your readers one sales letter after another. You'll have your valued readers looking forward to more if you include vignettes written in the flow of your own conversational voice, with bits of your life experience, peppered with insights, or questions your readers might enjoy answering.

Information about a topic you're researching is always interesting to followers of like-mind. Or perhaps you survey your readers, asking them to choose their favorite cover among two or three mock-ups for an upcoming book. You could share a character sketch of someone in the book you're currently working on, or simply chat about your writing process—barriers you've met, and triumphs you've won.

Be sure to include a clear means of opting out. Though you may not enjoy seeing people opt-out of receiving your communications, at the same time, you don't want them staying if your work isn't a fit for them. Some people will opt-in for a freebie and opt-out immediately after getting the freebie. That's fine, don't begrudge them. Your name, your work is in their world, and they may return one day. Secondly, when you consider that you pay for your email service according to the number of subscribers, there's no need to pay for anyone who is unengaged.

Some authors occasionally "clean" their list of subscribers who have not taken any action, while others do not, on the basis that inactive subscribers may yet become active.

So far I'm of the latter inclination, but it's an entirely individual decision, with no fault either way.

> *"Two questions form the foundation of all novels: 'What if?' and 'What next?'"*
> **Tom Clancy**

Giveaways

The act of giving away copies of your book, story, or partial is somewhat obviously referred to as "giveaways." In addition to Instafreebie, you'll see a lot of other giveaway opportunities as you get further into the indie author sphere. You can do your own individual giveaway, as well. There's a considerable amount of information on the internet from other authors about how they run their giveaways, using software such as Rafflecoptor.com, and other similar kinds of software that maintain the mechanics of giveaways.

Amazon also has giveaways, wherein you buy your own book and give away however many copies you wish. There are a couple of advantages in doing an Amazon giveaway.

The one of interest to me is that a simple giveaway can generate hundreds, and even thousands, of Amazon "followers" for you. The "Follow" button is on the Author page under the author picture. The only unfortunate aspect of Amazon's "follower" program is that they do not let authors have a clue as to how many—if any!—followers they have, let alone who they might be.

Yet another of those eternal mysteries of the great Zon. Of course Amazon knows, down to an eyelash, how many followers each and every author has. If any. Why not let us know?

Let us move on to consider the power points of your Amazon followers. Everyone who enters your giveaways is added to your Amazon followers list. And every one of them receives a personal email notice *every time* you publish a new book on Amazon. This is quite powerful, in my opinion. The emails are well done and if a follower is at all interested in your writing, whether fiction or nonfiction, they are likely to make the simple click that is a sale. There could be many clicks and many sales.

This is a wonderful thing. Yes, it's disappointing that Amazon doesn't let you know who these people are—in its determination to keep relevant statistics and information from authors—but you'll get a rough idea of how many *new* people are following you after a giveaway.

Here's an example: if you set up a giveaway to give away two copies of your ebook at $2.99 each, one to be given away for every 200 people who enter your giveaway, when both of your books have been claimed, you know that you have in the neighborhood of 400 new followers—for around $6.00, 70 percent of which you'll get back, of course, as that's your royalty. So, you'll pay 30 percent plus tax for the books you give away that are priced between $2.99 and $9.99, and 65 percent, plus tax, for books outside of that range. Very affordable advertising, with super affordable followers. *Utterly awesome!*

Gleam
With Gleam.io you can run giveaways, sweepstakes, competitions, grow your email list, increase your presence on social media, and more.

Lots of third party integrations and viral sharing. Plans run from free to $149.00 per month, with a really impressive free level—for example, unlimited competitions, unlimited entries, fraud protection, analytics, etc.

KingSumo
KingSumo.com is giveaway software that one purchases outright with no monthly fee. For $198.00 to $594.00 you get a Wordpress plugin, with a 60 day money back guarantee. If you believe you might go full force into giveaways, this is a good option to consider.

They have a focus on email list building, which is not available with Gleam's free option, but kicks in at a higher level.

There are other giveaway apps, too, but Gleam and KingSumo seem to lead the pack. There's likely to be more competition in giveaway apps as authors come to understand that books do not sell themselves, and buzz must be generated. Thus an occasional search for giveaway software may prove to be beneficial.

*"It ain't whatcha write,
it's the way atcha write it."*
Jack Kerouac

Your Book Launch

There's a considerable amount of information on the internet from the authors I mention below about *"The Book Launch."* Done right and with adequate planning, a book launch can send a book into the stratosphere, metaphorically speaking. There are a number of components to a book launch, and it's best accomplished with a lot of planning.

But there's also a steep learning-and-experience curve to book launches, so be patient, take your time, and, even if the publication of your book seems to have landed upon the moon with no fanfare, appreciate, at the very minimum, these two things:

1. You will get better and learn more about book launches as you continue your author journey

2. You can always re-launch your book

Say, what? Yes, you can always re-launch your book. This is not something that has been done by traditional big publishers as they're always on to the "next big thing." But you are the captain of your ship. You can re-write your book if you wish, and you can re-launch your book if you so desire.

Oh, happy days!

Keywords
What are keywords?

A keyword is a word or a phrase connected to the ideas and topics that define, relate to, or clarify your content.

So, for SEO (search engine optimization) keywords are the words and phrases that your potential reader enters when doing a search on a subject of interest, typed or spoken into a search engine—Google, Foxfire, Safari, others and also, Amazon, the largest shopping search engine on planet earth.

Well, then, what are tags?

A tag may be the exact same word or phrase as the keyword, the (somewhat thin) difference is that a keyword is entered into a search engine to find your article, story, blog, novel, poem, etc., and a tag is a word or phrase you use on your website or your on book's detail page, etc., to describe the specific work.

So, a rather global way of thinking about the difference might be that keywords are on the outside (larger) looking in, and tags are on the inside (narrower). But, again, they may both be—and often are!—the same words.

In either case, they both deserve thoughtful consideration as you come up with them. What would you enter into a search if *you* were looking for the work you've produced? What might be someone else's pain point or curiosity, that they would use as search terms?

Dynamic Ad Activity

Amazon Marketing Services – AMS

Let's take a look at *Amazon Marketing Services* – ams.amazon.com. At present, it may be the winner in the "What's the Best Way to Get My Book Seen?" lottery. The fees to get your book seen are inexpensive, and the returns, in some cases, are quite significant.

Further, not only do you get to sell your book, you also get a feel for what people are interested in for very little, or perhaps no, money. The other advantage to keep in mind is that when people shop for a book on Amazon, they are already in the "store" where books are sold. Not so for Facebook or Twitter ads.

AMS is a "pay per click" advertising platform, which means you only pay when someone clicks on your ad. In most cases, unlike many other ad platforms, it's only a few cents. And by a few cents, I mean five to ten cents. You can (and probably will) make higher bids as you discover which ads are performing for you, and you want them to be seen with more frequency.

But you can readily see, if no one clicks on your ad, something needs to be tweaked. *For free*, you get to literally see that something about your ad *isn't clicking* with your potential audience.

And, if you *are* getting clicks, but no sales, then you get to move to the "what's not working with my book's detail or landing page?" question.

For these reasons, AMS is a great training ground, as well as an excellent way for your books to get exposure, and, if all goes well, a happy way to make a few bucks. Though perhaps not many. Take a look at AMS even if you're not ready to place ads, to get its paradigm clear in your mind so you can hit the ground running when you *are* ready.

Here's a thumbnail sketch of how Amazon ads work. AMS ads are keywords auction-based. You designate how much you're willing to pay to have your ad appear in the customer's search when someone types in one of your keywords. You will not likely pay the full amount you entered that you're willing to pay.

As it's an auction-style platform based on a customer's interest, you may make a lower bid. But if your ad is intriguing to customers and gets more clicks, making Amazon more money, your ad may well out-perform a competing ad with higher bids on keywords.

That's a simplistic overview, but it begins to give you an idea why an ad with lower bids on keywords may get more impressions. That's to say, will "win" the auction. Given that each ad can have up to one-thousand keywords (and most of my ads have one-thousand keywords—taking advantage of the "free virtual real estate"), that's a-lot, a-lot, *a-lot* of bidding and jockeying for position going on.

But it's all automated.

The most interesting part of AMS is that, as of this writing and at this time, AMS will *not* spend the money you've agreed to be willing to spend. Nor anywhere near it. A few of my ads perform very well, but my ad spend has never approached what I've allotted for it. Every author I've talked with or heard talk about AMS ads, or read about in blogs, says the same thing.

Like me, they all want to be able to scale up their investment, as the ROI is significant. But Amazon, as usual, knows something—and many things—about its inner workings that we can only guess at, as we patiently put up more ads in the hopes of augmenting success.

The foregoing may be somewhat mystifying if you've never done it. But, thankfully, there's an impressive, and absolutely *free*, AMS course, taking it little-bitty step by little-bitty step by Dave Chesson at this URL: kindlepreneur.com/ams-book-advertising-course. He is very clear in his instructional method, has a friendly and open teaching manner, and is easy to understand.

He uses the software, *KDPRocket*, a keyword tool app that he developed himself. This tool is lauded by many authors, and is appropriate for him to use when explaining how to put up effective AMS ads.

I will add, however, that so far I've been using the free Google keywords tool, (more about it further on) which is effective in helping reach my one-thousand keywords, in addition to the ones I gather from Amazon searches. If I *were* to buy a keyword tool, it would be Dave Chesson's. As of this writing, it's quite affordable, and it no doubt produces a better list, faster.

Facebook Ads

One aspect of Facebook ads – facebook.com/business/products/ads that I believe is particularly significant regarding the success of the ad is the "look alike" audience. You gather the list of people who are your most relevant followers, subscribers, and/or readers, and send this list to Facebook, asking them to match it with people with the same profile, from their vast database. What I've heard from authors who've taken advantage of this marketing option is that it can be quite effective.

When it comes to Facebook ads, there's so much information all over the internet, I can only encourage you to do your own research.

But I would recommend that you check out Mark Dawson's free video tutorials: selfpublishingformula.com/courses/

As Mark recommends, be conservative with Facebook ads. I've heard more stories of people rapidly sinking a lot of money into the ads, than stories of people being wildly successful. But the "wildly successful" stories are much more talked about.

Engage with pragmatic caution. You can always spend more, but you can't spend less!

Instagram

Instagram.com is owned by Facebook and when you run a Facebook ad, you have the convenient option of having it run on Instagram as well, if you choose.

It's still true that a picture is worth quite a few words, so why not take advantage of Instagram's huge popularity and place your ad on Instagram's platform as well? Instagram has over 400 million active users—and growing.

Interestingly, 75 percent of Instagram users are outside of the U.S. and 90 percent of Instagram users are under 35. Sixty percent of all Instagram users log in everyday, with 3.5 *billion* "likes," every, single, day!

My suggestion? Make like a kite, and ride on that wind.

Twitter Ads

Twitter – ads.twitter.com – has over 317 million active users, although twitter ads seem not to get raves for performance. Tweets with images get 78 percent more click throughs, 89 percent more "likes" and 150 percent more retweets. Twitter engagement has increased 200 percent, year after year. Why don't the ads work for writers? It seems they should.

Go to Joshua Smith's (alphageeek) (yes, three "e's") post about his approach to twitter.com ads: alfageeek.wordpress.com/2016/05/04/step-by-step-twitter-ads – it's quite a clever game plan.

Google Ads
I don't recommend running Google ads – google.com/adwords for books. In my experience, they don't perform. (If you have a different experience, I'd love to hear about it.) What's great about signing up for Google ads is that you then get to use their keyword tool to generate keywords for your book, and for your one-thousand AMS keyword ads.

As mentioned, I'm an advocate of using any free virtual real estate, and so I'm inclined to attempt to have one-thousand keywords for each AMS ad. That's a lot of work without a tool. When you sign on to Google adwords, they'll require credit card information, as the intention is you'll be placing ads. Though you'll not be spending any money to access the keyword tool, you need to fill in this info to gain access to the tool.

Pinterest

What are possible advantages of Pinterest.com for authors?

First of all, like all social media sites, Pinterest sends its own particular traffic to your site, your books. As Kirsten Oliphant noted on Jane Friedman's blog, Pinterest runs marathons, not sprints.

When established, your Pinterest may send hundreds of page views every day from your pinned posts, whether new or years old. Kirsten affirms that the residual effect of Pinterest can beat out other platforms as it passively sends you potential readers, around the clock.

She further makes the observation that Pinterest is an introvert's dream—you're not expected to interact. You can post and pin quietly. Of course relationships are established through interaction, but there are plenty of other sites for that.

Pinterest has a well-developed search feature, allowing for easily finding content. Furthermore, Google shows pins in searches and thus, your site can rise in Google rank if you have a strong presence in Pinterest.

Some ideas for writers using Pinterest: If you have any tips about writing, combine them with an image and link to your site. Have a board of your published works, and create pins about your characters, your setting, or any other aspect of your creation that can be visual and intriguing.

Produce pins with beautiful pictures and captivating quotes. When you set up your Pinterest, be sure to set up a business account, which provides analytics, to see which pins perform the best. And even better, you can embed pins and boards into your blog posts or sidebar on your website!

You might also consider joining group boards through Pin Groups to reach more authors and readers, without, again, a lot of time invested in interaction. Or you could even start your own group board.

YouTube

If you don't have a YouTube.com channel yet, why not claim yours? You can create anything from a simple video of stills with the Ken Burns effect (slow pan or zoom on images) applied to them while you read from your novel or nonfiction book, to conducting casual interviews with your writer friends and acquaintances, to full-on, movie-like, production.

YouTube is an open field, limited only by your imagination. You never know when some small video you've put up becomes viral, sending hundreds and even thousands of curious potential followers to your website. *It does happen!*

General Internet Presence

And then there are all the usual suspects for your web presence. I suggest, along with internet gurus who have been in deeper trenches and for longer than I, to have your domain claim to each. Yes, even if you're not active. I hope you recognize the chorus I've returned to—that one wants to take advantage of free virtual real estate.

Even if you don't twitter, why not set up your account so if one day you do want to tweet your shiny, new, book release, you have the name you want to tweet—it hasn't been grabbed by someone else—and you have an idea of how to move forward, rather than trying to learn an overwhelming amount of things at once. That is not a good game plan.

The same goes for Pinterest and Instagram. One day you may suddenly decide to develop them, and, again, you'll be glad you laid the groundwork, if you haven't already. Be sure to keep all the sign ups and passwords and miscellaneous information about all your connections in one safe and tidy folder. That's the voice of experience advising you, which I wish I'd had when starting out.

It's all in preparation for the day you're ready to launch your book in a flurry of fireworks in every direction!

> *"A writer is someone*
> *who has taught his mind to misbehave."*
> **Oscar Wilde**

Various Sites to Advertise Your Book

Bookbub

Bookbub.com – Even if you're new to the indie author world, you may have heard of BookBub—the "gold standard" of advertising sites. The huge problem is, it's very difficult to get them to offer a feature deal for one's book.

And there are those who suggest it's becoming more difficult because they've moved away from assisting indie authors, and apparently toward letting the big publishers buy their advertising spots. A Bookbub deal is also quite expensive. There's a wide range of fees for a book deal, depending on its genre and if it's free or a paid book for $1, $2, or $3. As of this writing, the fees range from $55 to $3,600.

However, everyone I've heard talk about their Bookbub deals reports that the ROI (return on investment) is several times the initial investment, as well as causing a significant rise in the ranking of the book on Amazon. An accepted Bookbub deal can move the needle of your writerly career from nearly invisible to quite visible. Your excellent book can ride the waves of success, and carry along with it the other books in its series.

Yet more reason to write a series, if you're writing fiction, or to write related books, if writing nonfiction.

Barring getting a Bookbub featured deal, you might try their advertising option. No restraints regarding the price of your book, no requirement for a certain number of reviews, or anything else. It's an auction-style ad platform with a Cost-Per-Thousand impressions model.

I prefer a cost-per-click model, but it's still worth keeping in mind that Bookbub is exposure to a highly selective reading audience. I read mixed responses among authors about Bookbub ads. If you decide to try it out, I wish you great success, and, as always, I'd be interested to hear about it.

Sites & Lists of Sites to Market Your Books
There is some redundancy on these lists, but I believe it's better to have the information more than once than not at all.

Special thanks to Derek Murphy for this list of lists – creativindie.com/1100-new-places-to-market-your-books. And be sure to visit: creativeindie.com for a veritable wealth of author-relevant information.

Dave Chesson has a list of 127 of the top book promotion sites, both free and paid – Kindlepreneur.com/list-sites-promote-free-amazon-books and other author tools at Kindlepreneur.com, including KDPRocket, for great keywords.

Paid Author's list of Best Book Promotion Sites – paid-author.com/best-ebook-promotion-sites – Most of the listings on Paid Author have a discount code from 5 percent to 50 percent for paid listings, while many have free options.

Here are just a few of the listings on Paid Author's list, go there, or to one of the other listings for active links:
Free Booksy
Bargain Booksy
Books Butterfly
Book Runes
Pretty Hot Books
Kindle Book Promotion
Fussy Librarian
Robin Reads
The eReader Cafe

Book Bot Bob and Book Bot Bill – BookBotBob.com – is a Facebook messaging blast.

Author Marketing Club – authormarketingclub.com – Lots of free and paid author marketing tools and book promotion.

Awesome Gang Newsletter – awesomegangnewsletter.com – Lots of indie writer information and a free book listing.

Bookbongo – bookbongo.com – Free book promotion.

Book Daily – Bestsellers and BookDaily Author Update bookdaily.com – Writerly information and a fee-based book listing.

eBookLister – eBookLister.net – Free and paid book listing.

The Kindle Book Review – thekindlebookreview.net

Book Marketing Tools – bookmarketingtools.com – Lots of book marketing tools.

The 100 Best Websites for Writers – thewritelife.com/100-best-websites-for-writers-2017/

Sumo – sumo.com – Free and fee-based tools for your website growth.

Copyblogger – copyblogger.com, has a focus on teaching content marketing.

Self Published Author by Bowker – bowker.com – Here's where you buy your ISBNs in the U.S. Bowker also has other publishing tools and author information.

Patreon – patreon.com – A membership site for you to interact with your fans.

> *"To write is human,*
> *to edit is divine."*
> **Stephen King**

Helpful Indie Authors Blogs & Podcasts

Following are a few of my favorite indie author-related blogs and podcasts. Podcasts are great as they not only provide cutting-edge information, but they can be listened to when accomplishing other tasks, or at the end of the day when you're winding down.

They give a thumbnail sketch of what's happening in the Indie Publishing World, along with fascinating interviews with generous and intelligent writers who openly share valuable information that may save you literally *years* of uphill, trial-and-error learning and labor. Here are a few of my favorites:

Joanna Penn – thecreativepenn.com – Heading my list is Joanna Penn, who, along with her blog and helpful books for indie authors, has a weekly podcast, jam-packed with publishing information. Writers around the world look forward to her positive perspective on the indie ever-changing environment, and her fascinating interviews with notable personalities.

Brilliant, insightful, charming, and utterly transparent regarding her own writerly experience, Joanna has single-handedly done more than can be measured for the indie movement, encouraging unity, supporting advancement, maintaining good nature, and with it, wonderfully "infecting" the indie community. Her generosity of time and thoughtfulness is an outstanding role-model. She has done much to grow and sustain the warp and woof of the indie movement all over the world.

And, as if that's not enough, Joanna is also a talented, best-selling, fiction author with an ever-growing inventory of novels.

Mark Dawson – selfpublishingformula.com – Mark has a weekly podcast, co-hosted by James Blatch with intriguing guests. He also teaches outstanding courses on the sometimes seemingly arcane workings of Facebook and AMS ads, as well as host of a number of genre specific

Facebook Groups. Much sharing of insider information. *Excellent!*

Mark has written several books on the business of writing, as well as a slew of extremely successful novels.

Derek Murphy creativindie.com – This fascinating and brilliant young man bears mentioning again. Derek's website and YouTube videos are overflowing with vast amounts of information. And, in addition, I enjoy the guileless transparency of this Renaissance man.

The Sell More Books Show Podcast – sellmorebooksshow.com – Hosted by Bryan Cohen of Build Creative Writing Ideas, build-creative-writing-ideas.com, and Jim Kukral, of Author Marketing Club, author.marketing.club.com. A recap of the indie world of publishing every week—up to the minute, entertaining, and thoughtful.

Kobo Writing Life – kobo.com/writinglife – Mark Lefebvre or others at Kobo interview interesting, financially successful, authors.

Science Fiction & Fantasy Marketing Podcast – www.marketingsff.com – Hosted by Lindsay Buroker. Lots and lots of great information and great podcast interviews with genre authors and others in the indie movement.

Tom Corson-Knowles – tckpublishing.com – Tom interviews authors and significant influencers in the indie publishing universe on his podcast, and offers much helpful information on his blog. Further, Tom's publishing arm,

TCK Publishing, is interested in a wide range of writing, the primary requirements being good writing and a well-prepared submission.

The Rocking Self Publishing Podcast – rockingselfpublishingpodcast.com – Hosted by Simon Whistler, who has interviewed many indie authors. However, he's announced his "retirement" from the podcast, but you might be interested in listening to the show's archives.

Nick Stephenson – yourfirst10kreaders.com – Your **First 10,000 Readers**. Free guide to "Reader Magnets"—advocating permafree books to hook readers and build your list.

David Gaughran – DavidGaughran.wordpress.com – David is the author of *Let's Get Digital* and *Let's Get Visible*, and a long-standing champion of the indie author scene. Be sure to read his blog.

Steve Scott authority.pub – Steve has written several helpful books for the writing life and hosts an occasional podcast, although it appears, at present, to be on hiatus.

Iain Rob Wright – azofselfpublishing.teachable.com – AZ of Self-Publishing. Just when I think I'm about to hit "publish" on this book, something else comes out of the cosmos that demands inclusion for the beginning indie author. This new discovery, (thank you, David Gaughran) of Iain Rob Wright, blows everything out of the water.

Here are a few titles from the *well over one-hundred units* in Iain's completely free AZ of Self-Publishing course:

Why Self Publish?
Preparing Your Manuscript
Publishing on KDP
Audio
Creating Your Paperback
Building Your Website
Building Your Mailing List
Social Media
Promotion
Other Income
Advertising

This is an amazing compendium of free instruction and experience-driven insight from this charming, generous, transparent, and best-selling, Midlands, England horror author.

Reedsy – reedsy.com – Located in London, England, Reedsy provides vetted editing, design, website-building, publicity, and marketing resources.

This book would not be complete without mentioning Kristine Kathryn Rusch – kriswrites.com, and Dean Wesley Smith – deanwesleysmith.com, two beautiful and brilliant writers who have, together and individually, done more than can be measured for the authorial universe. Their offerings are so vast, they exceed the confines of this book. Go to their websites to begin to understand the range of their talent and commitment. Thank you, Kris and Dean.

Reviews

Generally speaking, a few reviews will help a book launch more successfully.

However, I no longer give reviews the attention I used to. I've had more reviews taken down, apropos of nothing I can comprehend, than I presently have on all my books.

For some arcane reason, Amazon will not allow one of my books to have over a dozen reviews. It's frustrating of course, but it's also curiously fascinating. The attention (or whatever it is) on an innocent YA novel is most peculiar. I've asked KDP several times about this oddness, and their only answer is, "well, it's not people, it's bots." Hmmm, yes, bots. But ... *why?*

While, conversely, my best selling book, as of this writing, has only five reviews.

I had an interesting conversation with a KDP employee who told me she feels reviews are not important. She said that in her experience, the only people who are concerned about reviews are writers. She works with customers as well, and she said not one single customer has *ever* mentioned reviews in any way—good, bad, or indifferent, while she has the discussion with writers on a daily basis.

This led me to decide that it's a healthy idea to take the thoughts and concerns from reviews and apply that energy to writing. (Though if you write a warm-hearted review of any of my books, not only will I be delighted, but Iain Rob Wright affirms that every time a kind review is written, a puppy is rescued from a well. So ... two good deeds-in-one.)

If you have beautiful reader comments, and Amazon doesn't remove them, that's excellent. May it continue to be so. My intention here is to encourage writers who have had a sad and frustrating experience with reader comments inexplicably removed.

You might occasionally look over your reviews and copy those you care about. Many authors have been shocked to see comments simply *gone* that were lovely, insightful, and relevant. If you've copied them, you can put them on your book's detail page—not only on Amazon, but on any site where your books are sold.

The review system is badly abused, and always will be. As long as reviews have inappropriate power, there will be those who will figure out a way to game the system.

The best revenge is winning. *And writing the next book is winning.*

In Closing

No doubt I've left out as much as I've put in. You may wonder why I didn't mention this person or that site—it may be because I don't know of them. It may be I felt it redundant. It may be because my experience with them has been less than ideal. However, I'm completely open to your feedback, and interested in your thoughts on what I've included in *Write Your Book! Publish Your Book! Market Your Book!*, as well as what I've not included.

My singular goal is that you honor and nurture your genius, that you share with the world your stories, your insights, your inspiration. If some of the bumps in your road are smoothed out with the tools and information I've placed at hand in this book, my mission will have been accomplished.

Now then, go *Write Your Book!*

Caveat on Everything Herein

No guarantees, just a list of resources, tools, and musings that I hope will advance your writerly/artistic life. If you're considering buying a product or service I've mentioned, as always, buyer beware. Do your due diligence.

I want to hear about any experience you've had with the information herein, if particularly good or particularly *not* good. I'm also interested in what you've learned and how your writing is going:
Blythe@BlytheAyne.com

Keep your candle burning....

Much gratitude to Pixabay and the generous photographers/artists on Pixabay for use of their images.

A Few Terms....

Trad - Traditional Publication, by, most often, a big New York publisher, but also generally includes university presses and other fairly large publishers.

Indie Publication – Independent publication by the author, or perhaps another indie author who has established a small press, offering support and certain skills needed by indie authors.

In the indie movement, small presses do not take money up front, except for, perhaps, specific skills, agreed upon by both the author and publisher. A few indie and small presses pay a small advance. Many do not, but they all will produce your book and get it in front of its potential audience.

Vanity Publication – Vanity publishers charge authors significant fees to produce and print books.

There are presses that ride the slippery-slope of vanity, attempting to pose as indie. *BEWARE*, dear author. Pay for nothing without first checking out the competition, doing price comparisons, and interfacing with peer indie authors. The Indie Movement is generous and protective.

Organizations such as ALLi (Alliance of Independent Authors), and SFWA (Science Fiction Writers of America), are relatively powerful, and quite protective of Indies. Query them about fees if any seem out of line or unethical.

References & Resources:

Write Your Book
Software:
Scrivener – *LiteratureandLatte.com*

Inspiring, Helpful Books:
Story Physics and *Story Engineering* by Larry Brooks

Writing Down the Bones by Natalie Goldberg

Marry Your Muse by Jan Phillips

Bullies, Bastards & Bitches – How to Write the Bad Guys by Jessica Page Morrell

Take off your Pants! by Libbie Hawker (perspective – you must plot)

Publish Your Book:
Wordpress.org – self-hosted, preferred path

Wordpress.com – Wordpress hosted, less autonomy and less preferred

Kobo Writing Life – *kobo.com/writinglife*

iBooks/iTunes Producer – *bookcreator.com/2013/11/publish-itunes-step-2-install-itunes-producer/*

Draft2Digital – *draft2digital.com*

KDP – *Kindle Direct Publishing*

Amazon's Author Central – *authorcentral.amazon.com*

ALLi – The Alliance of Independent Authors – *allianceindependentauthors.org*

Cover Artists – *https://insights.bookbub.com/fantastic-book-cover-design-resources/*

Mailchimp – *Mailchimp.com*

Mailerlite – *Mailerlite.com*

Bluehost – *bit.ly/hostblu*

Market Your Book:
Indie & Small Press Book Marketing by William Hertling

Let's Get Digital and *Let's Get Visible* by David Gaughran

Business for Authors,
How to be an Author Entrepreneur,
How to Make a Living with Your Writing,
How to Market a Book and
The Successful Author Mindset by Joanna Penn

The Miracle Morning for Writers,
How to Write a Nonfiction Book in 21 Days and
How to Discover Best-Selling Nonfiction eBook Ideas
by Steve Scott

How to Write a Sizzling Synopsis, by Bryan Cohen

* *

"I sense strongly that this world is a thin place indeed, simply a veil over a brighter and more amazing truth. To me, every ant, cloud, and star seems to proclaim that there is more to existence than we know."
Stephen King

About the Author

Here's a thumbnail sketch about me….

I live in a forest with a few domestic and numerous wild creatures, where, under my legal name and a couple of pen names, I create an ever-growing inventory of novels, short stories, illustrated kid's books, nonfiction books, articles, greeting cards, posters, and, yes, even wood carving when I need a change of pace.

I received my Doctorate from the University of California at Irvine in the School of Social Sciences, majoring in psychology and ethnography. I've always been filled with wonder, contemplating how people think and feel, and what beliefs and actions arise from those thoughts and feelings.

After I submitted my doctoral dissertation, I moved to the Pacific Northwest to write and to have a modest private psychotherapy practice in a small town not much bigger than a village. I had the privilege of working with amazing people, and I witnessed astounding emotional, psychological, and spiritual, healing. It was a wonderful experience.

But after twenty plus years, I realized it was time to put my focus on my writing, where, through the world-shrinking internet, I could "meet" greater numbers of people. *Where I could meet you!*

Your purchase of my work helps support this little corner of the earth, ten acres of natural forest and all its resident fauna. All the creatures and I thank you!

I Wish You Happiness, Health, Peace, and Joy,
Blythe

Questions, comments, observations? I'd love to hear from you!:

Blythe@BlytheAyne.com

www.BlytheAyne.com

www.ingramcontent.com/pod-product-compliance
Lightning Source LLC
Chambersburg PA
CBHW071738080526
44588CB00013B/2083